THE STREETWISE GUI

BUYING
SELLING
YOUR HOME

MARTIN VILLAGE

About the author

Martin Village went to Cambridge and Brussels Universities and worked as a barrister before participating in the eighties property boom. He is in his early forties and still deals in property as well as being a publisher of fine prints. He lives in London with his wife and two children.

THE STREETWISE GUIDE TO

BUYING &
SELLING
YOUR HOME

MARTIN VILLAGE

PIATKUS

Dedication

In memory of my father, Malcolm Village, who taught me a thing or two.

Acknowledgements

I am grateful to Robert Moser, a conveyancing solicitor, and to my brother, Peter Village, a planning barrister, for help with various aspects of this book.

First published in Great Britain
in 1987 by Judy Piatkus (Publishers) Ltd
5 Windmill Street, London W1

This revised and updated edition first published in 1993.

The moral right of the author has been asserted

A catalogue record for this book is available from the British Library

ISBN 0-7499-1270-7

Designed by Paul Saunders
Photoset in Linotron Times by
The Professional Data Bureau, London SW17
Printed and bound in Great Britain by
Biddles Ltd, Guildford & King's Lynn

CONTENTS

PREFACE

I am responsible for any gremlins that have found refuge in these pages, though it is ultimately a matter for your own judgement or that of your professional adviser as to whether in your particular situation you decide to follow my advice.

Being streetwise means knowing enough not to be afraid of tight situations or bemused by the mystique surrounding professional people you hire to work on your behalf. This book is not designed to save you the £300 or so in solicitor's fees by telling you how to do your own conveyancing. Instead, it will give you the survival skills you will need now that you are entering a world which, while retaining a thin veneer of respectability, can easily degenerate into the commercial equivalent of tag-wrestling. It is all about half nelsons, Boston Crabs, the brutal submissions and knock-outs of the property world. It is about not taking no for an answer, and about picking up the conductor's baton and getting your rag-bag of professional advisers to play a harmonious tune. You do not have to be an expert on every instrument, but it helps to know what key they are playing in.

INTRODUCTION

WHOOPS! THERE'S BEEN A SPOT OF UNPLEASANTNESS

Just a bit. You would have had to be only just this side of comatose not to have realised that something had gone very wrong with the housing market in the early 90s. Prices in parts of the South East dropped 30 per cent and though the rest of the country fared better in percentage terms, in real terms prices elsewhere didn't have as far to fall. Try digesting the following statistics:

● The boom peaked in 1988 when 2.1 million property transactions were recorded. The most ever, ever. By 1991 the figure had dropped to 1.3 million and the total for 1992 was a shade over 1 million, reflecting a drop in activity of more than 50 per cent, back to levels not seen since the 70s. Not in this century has there been a comparable boom followed by such a vicious downturn.

● At the end of 1992 more than 3 per cent of all mortgage borrowers were more than six months behind in their payments. This may not sound like much, but just look at the raw data. Since 1980 the number of people with mortgages rose from 6.2 to 9.8 million (another all-time high). Of these the largest number of households ever, 304,000, are more than six months behind with payments. Hundreds of thousands of other households, as many as one in ten, are feeling the pinch and, of course, these are problems that reverberate legally, medically and socially.

● You would expect the number of repossessions to rise during a period of high and rising unemployment. But though jobless figures have been higher, repossessions are running at unprecedentedly high levels, suggesting that even those in work can't keep pace. There were 75,000 homes repossessed in 1991, roughly the same figure as for 1992. Compare this with 3,500 for 1980.

- There are 250,000 unsold properties in the market. Some have been around for literally years and present an obstacle to recovery.

- A vast number of property owners, 1.5 million, are in the unfortunate position of having 'negative equity' in their property— a pompous way of saying that the value of their house is lower than the size of their mortgage. Many of the people experiencing this novel brand of dismay are in the 25-34 age group and took out big mortgages to fund their first ever property purchase.

- Anecdotal this, but some say that 25 per cent of all deals done in the recession in the South East have been subject to gazundering (a term which will be familiar to the streetwise among you and referring to the practice where the buyer offers less than the originally agreed price, usually at the point of exchange of contracts). The extent of what was once a relatively rare event underlines the degree to which the buyers' market has taken hold.

- Out of a total housing stock of around 23 million in 1991, a staggeringly high 1.3 million houses were reported to be unfit to live in.

SO WHAT WENT WRONG?

Practically everything you could think of, and some things no one thought of. A number of planets that had never before drawn up in alignment did so unexpectedly and with disasterous results for the UK.

The boom years created the ideal conditions for a really unpleasant downturn. In pursuit of her property-owning democracy, Margaret Thatcher encouraged everybody (council tenants in particular) to take on borrowings which only made sense in a rising property market. That very fun duo, low interest rates and readily available mortgage finance, came to the party, and it went with a swing (upwards). The morning after, the nation was left with a serious debt hangover.

Just at the time the government decided to put the brakes on inflation, a worldwide recession (worse by far in the English speaking world) hit the UK. Inflation would have fallen quite naturally without the imposition of deflationary policies, but to combine high interest rates with recession seems in retrospect to be almost inspired in its stupidity, like shooting yourself in both feet with one bullet. Prices began to fall. Small businesses, underpinned in better times by house prices, began to go under.

Unemployment rose. Repossessions sky-rocketed. Confidence evaporated. Prices fell further, and so the cycle repeated itself, gathering momentum. We finally got our reward of relatively low inflation, but no one was in a position to appreciate it. For every one percentage point fall in inflation, house values in the South East fell a clear 5 per cent.

Then there was the ERM. That was a great idea, but we blew it. By entering at too high a rate we ensured that interest rates would have to be kept high to maintain the pound's value within its ERM band. As we all know, high rates for a prolonged period had a devastating effect on the housing market. And all because John Major wanted the pound to be as strong a currency as the Mark (probably he still does)—an unfortunate piece of hubris this, given the labile state of the UK economy, and comprehensible only as a stray piece of 80s euphoria. Just look at the result. If interest rates hadn't fallen, Whitehall would've had to dust down the file marked 'What To Do When the Middle Classes Riot'.

The cost of German unification may, arguably, be felt in the pocket of every single citizen of Western Europe, which includes, of course, buyers and sellers of houses in the UK. The argument goes like this: in order to counter the inflationary effect of pumping massive amounts of new Marks into former East Germany (they were shipped down the autobahn by the lorry-load), and thereby bestowing on that blighted nation a standard of living which in Western economic terms it hadn't earned, the Bundesbank chose to keep monetary policy tight i.e. to maintain high interest rates. This meant, and means, pain elsewhere—particularly for the UK which, whether inside or outside the ERM, still has to watch the pound/Mark relationship with special care.

Can we question the conduct of anyone in particular?

Why not? Banks and building societies behaved no better than we have come to expect them to. They lent profligately on the basis of ever increasing house prices, then, when the market fell, they reacted by pushing repossessions to an all time high, very often with astonishingly callous indifference to the fate of their erstwhile borrowers.

But banks and building societies aren't entirely the villains of the piece. They play follow-my-leader. Step forward the leaders they followed. There were only ever three serious nominations in this category: Margaret Thatcher, Nigel Lawson and John Major. For their services, Thatcher and Lawson became Baroness and

Lord respectively. No one can say we are not a grateful nation. For Honest John Major, a similar fate is only a matter of time.

Can you enjoy the recession?

If you can enjoy the recession you can enjoy anything, and the answer is, you *can* enjoy the recession. There are compensations, admittedly of a dark and ironic order. During the boom, everyone was a closet developer. Now we're all closet economists. And it's a lot of fun. The buzz of guessing when the economy is going to turn is so much more exquisite when your house is on the line. And bad news is almost palatable when you can watch po-faced professional economists dissecting rattled and badly informed politicians on TV.

LONG-RANGE FORECAST

Dreary. Showers continuing intermittently until 1994, when we should begin to see an improvement, with brighter weather appearing first over the South East and spreading slowly northwards ....

After the slump, can we expect a boom? No. Boomlets, possibly, but nothing on the scale of the late 80s. Whether inside or outside the ERM, increasingly closer European economic integration will prevent UK governments, of whatever hue, from going off on frolics of their own. The prevailing mood of monetary austerity could continue, in face of the inflationary effects of the German East/West merger, for the rest of the decade.

Of course there are going to be regional and local variations, but the best guesses are that capital growth from 1993 onwards will average 6 per cent per annum. In actual terms, this means that it will be 1998 before people who bought at the height of the boom see the value of their houses regain their 1988 levels.

Will it be a buyers' or a sellers' market? A buyers' market until 1994; then something refreshingly new to the post-war generation; neither a buyers' nor a sellers' market, but a more balanced market in which the art of buying and selling will really begin to matter. Expect to hear of gazumpings and gazunderings happening side by side in the same street.

When will the market turn? Expect to see prices begin to rise in late 1993, as interest rates reach levels of 6 per cent. This is the point when it becomes cheaper (at present price levels) to have a mortgage than to pay rent. The opportunistic renters, sensing this, will pile back into owner-occupied accommodation.

If renting gets more popular, will it dent the market in owner-occupied housing? Not much. We need a healthy rental sector to act as a pressure valve for the freehold sector—it prevents the market from overheating and from prices rising out of control. Contrary to popular belief, the private rental market has done anything but thrive since Margaret Thatcher introduced the shorthold tenancy option (see page 94). It has actually shrunk by 3 per cent to an all-time low of 7 per cent of the housing stock. Expect this figure to rise by 3 per cent or so during the decade as rented accommodation from Housing Associations becomes more popular. It is salutary to ponder that within living memory (1950) well over 50 per cent of the housing stock was rented privately, with only 29 per cent owner-occupied and the rest in the public rented sector. Now the figures are 67.5 per cent owner-occupied, 7.4 per cent privately rented and 22 per cent in the public rented sector.

Can we expect demographic changes. Yes. A gradually ageing population will help prospects for youth employment which in turn will fuel demand in the vital first-time-buyers market. In addition, it is fashionable to have children again—for women the great age is 28 and young families are a potent force in housing demand. You can't live with your in-laws for ever or, in some cases, at all. Surprisingly, the 25-34 age group has not lost faith in the idea of home ownership and are set to come on strong.

Will there be problems along the way? You bet. There is the little matter of 225,000 unsold properties overhanging the market at the beginning of 1993 and more on the way. In addition, the system has in-built dampeners, known as valuers, whose anxiety to protect the interests of their clients (banks and building societies) by low valuations manages to scupper about a quarter of all deals. The neuroses and self-imposed inhibitions of the lenders will be sufficient to ensure that the recovery will be gradual.

Does the North-South Divide still exist? Yes it does, so don't let anyone tell you it has disappeared. No such luck. While the pain and anguish has been most acute in the South East, the North has by no means escaped unscathed and prices there, remember, were lower to start with. Average regional prices tell their own story. The North weighs in at £47,000 (having hit a high of £50,000 in 1990); but accommodation in Greater London is still the most expensive at £81,000 (down from a high of £87,000). As motorways become more crowded, and as British Rail ceases to exist as an effective transporter of commuters, the South East will forge ahead.

CLOUDS AND SILVER LININGS

Selling

We are not stupid, we are sensible. Everyone knows that a falling market is a bad time in which to sell, and will avoid doing so if they have any choice in the matter. Thus it is that 50 per cent of potential sellers have in the last two years, quite literally, stayed at home. This pent-up desire to move (very strong in the English— we do it an average of four times in our lives) will eventually find expression when the market turns—late '93, and all of '94 look propitious. For those who have no choice in the matter (debt and divorce being the most common motives), here are a few tips:

• Remember that if you have to sell, that is precisely what you are trying to do, not give your house away. Nothing undermines your chances more than the appearance of desperation—which may, oddly, undermine your chances of ever selling at all. The rider to this is that the price when you hit the market must, crucially, be priced to sell. Don't imagine that you can reduce the price after a while and still achieve the same impact. The first month of marketing is the most vital and is the time when most acceptable deals are done. There will be buyers out there who have seen everything on the market and are waiting for something to get excited about.

• Get to know the market yourself. Go round all the agents and discover how much comparable properties have sold for and when. You can then conduct informed conversations with agents and buyers alike. (See Agents, page 116)

• Go for maximum coverage from the outset and appoint more than one agent, so that at best you will get competing offers (gazumping went on even in the depths of the recession); at worst you will find the one buyer with whom you can do business.

• Try to maintain a healthy scepticism in the face of offers from people with places to sell—which does not mean that you should turn down an offer, but never under these circumstances take your house off the market. It is a fact that there are many so-called buyers around who have no concentrated intention of buying. They are poking about and making mischief. Others imagine that they can sell their own place (question them closely about this and make your own assessment of the chances of sale). Very often there is a yawning gulf between their optimism and harsh reality. (See Grilling the Buyer—page 64)

• There are gazunderers and gazunderers. There are the 'honest' sort and the bloody-minded variety—the latter oddly enough being sometimes easier to deal with than the former. (See page 68)

• Never has it been more important to present your property to its best possible advantage, but that does not mean that in your anxiety you should go in for extravagant 'improvements' which will simply deepen the hole in your pocket without significantly improving your chances of sale. Essential repairs are a greyer area. Obviously, minor cosmetics, such as a pot of paint judiciously applied, can be cheap and effective, but new roofs are expensive and on the balance of risk it may be more sensible to leave some decisions to the new owner. After all, price advantage is what buyers, fundamentally, want. (See chapter 5 on Selling)

• Finally, if you're fortunate enough to have made a sale, but not quite for the price you were expecting, you will not have despaired, will you, because you will have ensured that the place you were buying was commensurately cheaper?

Buying

The logic is shattering. When it's a bad time to sell it must be a good time to buy. At the back of all your dealings is the knowledge that no one sells in a recession unless they have to, and accordingly, the pickings have never been easier, though not necessarily richer (too many potential sellers of better properties are biding their time). Nevertheless, there are lots of new places to look to find bargains—banks and building societies are now huge repositories of repossessed property, and are likely to remain so for the rest of the decade (see page 23.) And not for years have there been so many country houses on the market at (relatively) affordable prices, sometimes at half the price they commanded at the height of the boom, courtesy of Lloyds losses and the white-collar recession.

The golden rule must nevertheless be that you should never buy a place on price factors alone—buy a house because you like it, and because of its intrinsically desirable qualities. Sensible buying makes selling—in whatever economic climate—so much easier.

Tastes are fickle and the indications are that the racier and trendier mood of the 80s is definitely out. So, with an eye for re-sale, you might want to avoid, this time round, conversions from industrial and institutional buildings (wharves, mills, churches and railway stations); barns are borderline and will depend on the quality of the original conversion. Out, too, are executive homes on newly built estates—the cause of much negative-equity-inspired misery. In come family houses of character—purpose-built and solid.

Finally, amid the endless opportunities to talk prices down (see chapter 3), bear in mind that it would be a mistake to treat the property market as though it was still the fast moving bazaar of the boom years. Houses, unlike stocks and shares, are designed to be lived in, and they tend to move too slowly, particularly in a declining market, for money to be made 'on the way down' in a reliable and organised way. The word is, buy sensibly and buy as though you mean to live there; and never buy anything you won't be able to resell in existing market conditions.

IMPONDERABLES

Just to make us feel good, just to make us feel that little bit more relaxed about bricks and mortar, let us take comfort from the thought that, although economic retrenchment may cause us to live on such comestibles as smoky bacon crisps, Kentucky Fried Chicken and Mogadon, the housing market will march forever on. There'll be all the more reason to have a roof over your head when the giant ozone hole opens up at all points north of Watford. And for Londoners, when traffic grinds to a final terrible halt (stress levels having reduced the sperm count of its male citizenry to almost zero) there will still be a need for more substantial accommodation than three sides of a cardboard box. Towards the end of the decade, embrace the prospect of a collective millenarian hysteria which causes people to look with increasing interest at housing close to or on well-appointed hills. Being streetwise you will have already secured your space....

Now, read on.

STRATEGY

'Timing is everything'.

Chubby Checker

1

GET READY—
FINDING THE PROPERTY

WHICH AREA?

Whether you pull yourself up by your own bootstraps, or are in the happy position of having money at your disposal or owning a place already, you will still have to know not only how to look, but what to look for and what to avoid.

In the cautious 90s never has it been more important to buy property in safe, uncontroversial areas. This is not the era of the pioneer—as arguably was the case in the 80s—and if you buy in an area with a rough reputation, hoping that it will 'come up', you may be in for a long wait.

There are exceptions—such as parts of London where it is accepted that barrister may live next to burglar and where litter and the whoop of police sirens are accepted as part and parcel of life in the capital. Close proximity to a park or open space, a good school for the kids, transport for getting to work, an area of solid reputation — all these things will support the price of the place you buy and make it easier to sell once you move on. And in financial terms you make more money in the 'solid' area than in the one that has been 'discovered', because, quite simply, the same percentage increase on a more expensive property is clearly going to be worth more in cash terms than a similar percentage increase on a less expensive property.

Unless they are really gross and obtrusive, any apparent disadvantages in the immediate vicinity of a London property (also Bristol, Bath, Winchester, Oxford, Cambridge and any nice town south of Watford) will translate themselves not so much into lower prices, but more in terms of the difficulty of finding the 'right' buyer. A property located right next to a public urinal, or a 24-hour warehouse, or a railway line will probably fetch the same price as one slightly farther away from the offending blemish, but it may well take longer to sell. Of course, you may say, time is money and on that basis a property which takes longer to sell, even at the same price as a similar property, is worth marginally less.

The rule in the suburbs and the countryside is unchanged: anything that threatens to disrupt the peace and tranquillity of a residence will usually be reflected in price. Location is vital. You move to the country to escape the kind of environment that prevails in the city. If, once you get there, you still find you are having to wade knee-deep through litter in the streets of your country town, jostle shoulder to shoulder with burglars, pick-pockets and roughnecks, or suffer noise and pollution from cars or trains, then there is hardly any point in dislocating yourself. You might as well stay in town where the shops are better and everything is more 'convenient'.

The country also seems to pose its own problems: farming is an industry with its own effluents, noises and smells, and you should think twice before you buy a cottage next to one. Also, have you noticed how the nicest parts of the countryside, particularly in the eastern part of the country (but we shall not forget Salisbury Plain) seem to have been requisitioned by the Army or the Air Force? You are as likely to run into a Chieftain tank at the bottom of your dingly dell as you are a tractor or another car. And what residents and sellers of idyllic thatched cottages will not tell you is that above the permanent mist of fertiliser, jet planes practise dogfights in the clouds and you might as well live on an airstrip at Heathrow. Avoid buying anything near to a sinister and well-guarded 'Defence' establishment (you never know what they are making), an atomic power station or anything remotely nuclear. Finally, if the rural peace is to be broken by nothing else you can usually depend on shotgun blasts to do the job, blowing holes in foxes, rabbits and pheasants in time-honoured style. And you may even be allergic to the twitter of birdsong. If it is peace and quiet you want, you might very well decide to stay in town.

For information gathering, shopkeepers are often a gold-mine, as are publicans, particularly in country villages. If you drink, you can do worse than spend a few judicious pounds at what may become your local. If, when leaning at the bar you are asked to sign the petition protesting at the siting of a low level nuclear waste dump nearby, you may think again. If buying in a part of the country you find attractive but are not really familiar with, stay in a hotel for a week and take it all in.

The crucial point for you, as buyer, is: if there are any drawbacks or disadvantages to a particular property or the particular area in which it is located then that should give you greater scope for negotiation on the price in a private sale. This is more difficult in the overheated London market, but easier to do in the suburbs or the country.

WHICH HOUSE?

There are various options open to you as ways of finding your dream house.

Knocking on doors

In the UK there are well over 20 million front doors to knock on, so be selective. If you see a street you like, be impulsive, ask around to find out who owns what, whether anyone in the neighbourhood wants to sell. Remember, people initially feel threatened by strangers appearing at the door, so do not dress offensively; make yourself appear gullible, pleasant and open.

Very rarely will the owner turn you away, and particularly not in a recession. You may get a warmer reception than you bargained for. If you like, begin your patter with a profuse apology, 'I know it's late—I just happened to be in the area, and I do apologise...' Just possibly, if the house has a 'For Sale' sign outside, the seller may have given explicit instructions for visitors to come through the agent, in which case you may be told to go away and come back through the 'proper' channels. The usual reason for this is burglar paranoia. These days the streetwise burglar bent on this form of reconnaissance will go through the agents like anyone else. Before you slope off hand the seller your card or a piece of paper with your name and address. You can even have one printed up. You must be straight if you give that out, and you never know your luck, you may get some response. Usually the sellers will be glad to show you round, either because they are more polite than you or because the agents have not sent anyone round for weeks.

If you like the house and eventually make an offer you can give the seller the option of a 'private deal', whereby he will avoid paying an agent's commission fee, though sellers should watch out for agreements with agents where commission is payable in the event of any sale whether through the agent or otherwise.

Local and national papers

This is the quickest way to contact sellers directly and without the need for going through agents. Serious private sellers, deliberately wishing to avoid paying agents' fees, will be advertising in local papers for the country, national papers for both town and country.

Look through the property pages of *The Times* and the *Telegraph* every Wednesday, and on Sunday, the *Sunday Times*, the *Sunday Telegraph* and the *Observer*. The *Financial Times* on a Saturday charges high rates, and generally advertises only the most expensive houses.

Placing a 'want to buy' advertisement in a national paper is expensive and usually a waste of time. It is dangerous to be too specific—you might exclude some perfectly good house. All you will do is attract a flood of replies from estate agents and one can do that a lot cheaper by contacting them directly. For some reason advertising in local papers seems to bring better results. Also it is considerably cheaper.

Finally, keep your eyes open for details of auctions, when and where they take place.

Agents

Cover all of the agents in the area and get on as many lists as you can. Even if the deal you are doing is private, it is vital that you get to know the local market thoroughly. In two weeks of reading sheaves of agents' particulars you should be as expert as anyone, and will be able to value a house or flat yourself to within 5 or 10 per cent of its market price. If you tangle with agents read chapter 11 to see what these people really get up to.

Your current address?

The best deal you ever did may well be your very first if you are able to buy a place at an advantageously low price by virtue of your special status. So, if you are reaching towards the first rung of the property ladder ask yourself whether you are:

● a council tenant with a right to buy

● a sitting tenant with Rent Act protection

● a leasehold tenant with a right to buy the freehold under the Leasehold Reform Act.

If your luck is in, turn to chapter 4 (page 40) for details of how to proceed.

Approaching institutions

Almost any institution which owns land and houses will be in the market in some guise—either to sell freeholds, leaseholds or to rent. By digging around and persevering, you can come up with some exotic buildings. Here are a few ideas, but the list is by no means exhaustive:

Breweries These are traditional holders of residential housing, and every time the directors decide to rationalise or increase liquidity some of their housing stock hits the market.

Forestry Commission The Commission sometimes sells cottages, coach houses and building land, though you might find yourself surrounded by pine forest.

Church Commissioners The Church of England, next to the Crown, is the wealthiest landowner, and the Church Commissioners are the hired hands that deal with Mammon. Anything from vicarages, redundant churches, to very classy housing at the top end of the market (in recent years they have sold off most of Maida Vale). Like many other big landowners not exempted from the strictures of the Leasehold Reform Act, they have adopted a policy of sell rather than rent, and are very deal oriented. Charity is the last thing you should expect.

British Rail BR have orders to sell off all extraneous landholdings, and it is sometimes possible to discover a disused station or goods yard which you can convert or develop as the case may be. You can get good deals from BR, they sell land at agricultural prices (£2000 an acre or less).

Oxford and Cambridge colleges Their position is very similar to the Church of England. The bursars now manage portfolios of investments, from property through stocks and shares. They employ agents who are not known for their flexibility or charm, and do not imagine that because they are academics they have their heads in the clouds and are thinking about Sophocles and the Origin of the Universe.

Save Britain's Heritage If you are in the market to restore a historic building, contact these people. They have details of most of the important buildings that are under threat (see also page 159), and will vet you to see if you are capable of taking one on. An adoption agency for needy buildings.

Banks and Building Societies have plenty of repossessed property on their books—there were 75,000 repossessions in 1992—for sale at knock-down prices. Approach these institutions directly, but don't expect them to move fast or for any ensuing deal to be trouble-free. The leviathans of the property world, building societies are slow-moving, often unresponsive bureaucracies. In addition, the mortgagee-in-possession (the bank or building society) may be rowing in a different direction to the legal owner who, although dispossessed, remains just that, the legal owner, and may be feeling understandably unco-operative. A recent legal case decided that lenders have a duty to resell property quickly and may be liable for losses caused by any delay. It remains to be seen whether this landmark decision will have any effect on the notoriously slow reaction time of the big institutions. Having said that, it is worth the hassle. There are enormous savings to be made on repossessed property.

The Land Registry is now open to the public so that, technically, you can find out who owns what in circumstances where ownership is unclear.

2

GET SET—PROCEDURE
AND LEGALITIES

If you are going to manipulate the rules, you must know your way round them. You will never be able to play the system to your best advantage unless you have some understanding of the legal landscape in which you will be operating. Also, remember that a little legal knowledge is a dangerous thing—for solicitors, that is, because you may have some idea what they ought to be doing.

Things move notoriously slowly, not only for bureaucratic reasons (for instance, the search can take ages to go through) but for more profound reasons.

You do not have to be cautious in buying a house, but you may have time to regret it if you are not. Unfortunately caution means checking details, asking questions, and this usually takes time. Secondly, there seems to be a feeling, common not only to lawyers but to the public at large, that a hurried sale is a dangerous one. Many buyers and sellers often need time to get used to the idea, and would not shoot from the hip even if they could.

Most people are understandably reluctant to move into a new house before they have sold their old one (the alternative is the dangerous business of 'bridging') and most sellers will not sell unless they have somewhere to go to.

The ugly truth is that unless you can take matters into your own hands a deal will be as slow as the slowest participant wants it to be. And if you are in a chain, that can be slow indeed.

But you can have your cake and eat it too. There are ways of steering a quick course through the legal morass, and equally, it may sometimes be to your advantage to slow the process right down (in which case the sluggishness of the system works in your favour).

The process of buying a house is known as 'conveyancing'. Very broadly, it involves the collection of information from the seller and the local authority which has responsibility for the area in which the house is located; an exchange of contracts, which is the flashpoint of the whole deal; and completion of the conveyance, which involves exchanging money and property.

MAKING THE OFFER

Making an offer and agreeing to buy is no more than an expression of goodwill—often a very necessary one—but fortunately not one that is legally enforceable, generally, speaking unless you want it to be.

It used to be the case that an unwitting punter could stitch himself up by making a written offer to buy or sell, and if this offer contained sufficient details to identify the parties, the property in question and the price, then the other party could simply write in reply 'I accept your offer', and this would have created a legally enforceable contract. Thus the practice of solicitors and agents to use the words 'Subject to Contract' on all property correspondence to guard against this. Old habits die hard, and we can expect to see this almost entirely redundant phrase crop up for a long time to come.

Under the Law of Property (Miscellaneous Provisions) Act 1989, the requirements for a legally binding contract are that the relevant terms of the transaction should be incorporated in one document signed by all parties, or in identical documents signed by each party and exchanged between the parties (the dreaded 'exchange of contracts'). It would, therefore be extremely difficult for you to commit yourself to a legally binding contact without meaning to, unless you were illiterate, terminally spaced out or both (and even then you could probably get out of it for the same reasons).

Once your offer is accepted, instruct a solicitor to get on with:

• Making preliminary enquiries

• Checking that the seller has good title to the property i.e. that he has the ability to sell to you

• Obtaining a local land charges search

• Agreeing the final form of the draft contract which will have been prepared by the seller's solicitor

• Making sure that your financial arrangements are in place (for example that you have an adequate mortgage offer, free of conditions with which you cannot comply)

- Arranging for contracts to be exchanged
- Completing the transaction.

You could, of course, just let the lawyers get on with it, but you are not yet home and dry, and only on exchange of contracts can you really afford to relax.

ASK AND YOU MAY BE TOLD: PRELIMINARY ENQUIRIES

The solicitor's first job is to discover precisely what it is you think you are going to buy, and preliminary enquiries are supposed to help in this process. In practice these enquiries have become debased. While the seller could be responsible for any outright lies communicated by a solicitor, stonewalling has nevertheless become a fine art. You can expect monosyllabic replies or stock answers such as 'not to the seller's knowledge'. At best, you might get some idea of the responsibilities that are likely to be yours in your new house.

Although it could take five minutes do not be surprised if the enquiries drag on for two or three weeks. They concern:

- the precise boundaries of the property, and who owns the boundary walls;

- whether there are or have been any disputes relating to the property;

- whether the property is subject to any local authority notices (typically relating to the state of repair of the building);

- whether there are any guarantees (damp, woodworm, dry rot, etc.) and what fixtures and fittings are included;

- what services are connected to the house (gas, water, electricity, mains drainage);

- whether there are any rights over the land;

- whether there are any outright restrictions on use;

- whether any planning permissions have been granted and if these have been adhered to.

CHECKING LEGAL TITLE

Checking legal title is straightforward and quickly done if the land is registered (most is). Entries on the Land Certificate will reveal who owns what and whether anyone apart from the seller has a legal interest in the property you are buying. If the land is unregistered your solicitor will have the unenviable task of wading through piles of conveyances stretching back into time. And if the property you are buying is leasehold someone (your solicitor) will have to read through the lease.

SEARCH AND YE SHALL FIND

The 'local land charges search' search is designed to give information about the planning history of the particular house—whether planning permissions have been given in the past and whether the terms of these have been complied with, and whether any work on the building has been carried out in line with building regulations. There may be 'enforcement notices' if the building work has taken place without permission, and 'closing orders' if the general state of the building offends any building or hygiene regulations.

The search also gives information, in a limited way, about the local authority's plans for the area as a whole. So if they propose to widen the road, or erect a flyover, or compulsorily purchase your house, it should turn up on the search. But unfortunately the system is not foolproof—the only plans included on the search are those sufficiently far advanced to warrant inclusion in the land charges register. The local authority may be toying with the idea of a new ring road passing within 20 feet of the house and you will simply not get to hear of it. The other major drawback of the search is that it does not reveal private applications for planning permission by neighbours, and it would not tell you, for example, whether the derelict site at the end of the road is to become a high-rise block, a multi-storey car park, a supermarket or pleasant residential housing. The only way to fill in the gaps in the search is to ask neighbours and, informally, the planning officer at the local authority (see also page 153).

When all other matters can be dealt with relatively quickly, a long wait for the search can cause you problems, particularly at a time when house prices are rising fast; a pause of up to three months can enormously increase the risk of your being gazumped. The seller may, quite justifiably in some cases, feel that the agreed sale price no longer reflects the true value of the house.

Guard against this if you can by exchanging 'subject to search'. The problem here is that if the seller is well advised, he may well not agree. As far as he is concerned there will still be a distinct possibility that you will avoid the deal if some aspect of the search is not to your liking; and meanwhile his hands will simply be tied and he will be unable to accept a higher offer if it comes along. The answer may lie with the property. If it is in reasonable shape and if the seller knows of no problems, you as buyer can say, why should there be any? If he refuses to exchange subject to search, you can suggest to him that his refusal amounts to a tacit admission that he has something to hide. Rather a cheeky thing to do, and at the back of it will be an implication that you might withdraw altogether if he does not exchange subject to the search. But it might be enough to hustle a vacillating seller into doing so.

Personal searches

When you finally lose patience with the local authority or where a gazumper appears on the scene, or, anyway, if you just want to move faster, most local authorities allow members of the public to carry out their own searches. You can either do it yourself or get a search agent to go through council records for you. Expect to pay around £100 plus VAT and plus the council's search fee, and demand that results be available in 48 hours, no later. This would be a complete answer to the problem of the late search if you were allowed to get answers to all your questions. Oddly, though, some departments of the local authority will not entertain personal searches. Planning seems to be okay, but you may have difficulty in discovering whether building regulations have been complied with or if any notices are in force on the property. And in the London region at least, the Environmental Health departments of various councils, for reasons best known to themselves, seem to be a complete no-go area for personal searches.

Matters of plumbing and sewerage may not be uppermost in your mind until, of course, you discover that the builder who converted the flat you bought on the strength of a personal search put a manhole in the wrong place.

As a result of the patchy nature of the information you are likely to get, some building societies refuse to advance money on the strength of a personal search. Check that yours will.

For use in emergencies, therefore. Remember that if the local authority gave you an incorrect answer, you could sue them for it—but if you mess up your personal search you have only yourself to blame.

EXCHANGE OF CONTRACTS—THE FLASHPOINT

All the while your solicitor will have been shuttling a contract back and forth to the seller's solicitor. The seller's solicitor provides the initial draft, and they then select different coloured pens and set about altering it to their satisfaction.

All your enquiries are out of the way, and you have in the meantime lined up your finance by way of a mortgage after a valuation survey. The seller has indicated his readiness to 'exchange' and it is all systems go.

Exchange of contracts is the critical point in the transaction. After exchange, by all means bring out the champagne. The house is yours, or more accurately, is bound to become yours.

The draft contract will usually be based on one of the standard forms supplied by law stationers, containing provisions which are generally applicable to most transactions. Sometimes the seller's solicitor will put in special conditions to cover a particular situation, for instance where part of a plot of land is being sold and the seller wants to retain some control over what the buyer does on it (e.g. only build one house; maintain boundary fences; allow the seller's drainage pipes to remain in place etc). There will be a clause in the contract which states that the buyer has not relied on anything said to him by the seller or his agents which has influenced him in his decision to buy the property, and that the buyer can only rely on written statements passing between the buyer's and seller's solicitors. This is very standard stuff and not worth a great argument. If the seller has said something which is important in the deal, make sure it is confirmed in writing by the seller's solicitor. If this causes a problem, start worrying.

Watch out for the clause which absolves the seller from liability for anything he may have said which turns out not to be true, but which induced you to make an offer or on which you relied in buying the house. You can try to get out of it, but the seller's solicitor will probably insist that it stay in. And if, of course, you are the seller you insist that it does.

A final word. If work remains to be done on the house at the time of exchange, you should, as buyer, get it written into the contract. For example: the seller has promised to provide a damp proof guarantee—make completion conditional on his producing one.

Insurance

Remember that as soon as you have exchanged contracts, you, as buyer, will be required to insure the house. If it burns down between exchange and completion, you still have to complete, and to pay over the agreed purchase price to the seller. This may seem strange because, obviously, the seller occupies the house until it is handed over—but it is the rule. There are moves to change this, and some contracts specify that the risk remains with the seller until completion, but banks and building societies will, in any event, require the buyer to insure as from exchange. If the seller deliberately damages the house between exchange and completion then technically he is liable to compensate you. There are enormous problems of proof (evidence of intent) here, and it is wiser to forget about civil action. If you really want to get your own back—imagine, for instance, that the seller has ripped out a marble fireplace—threaten to bring the police in and have charges of theft and criminal damage brought. You may also refuse to complete if you find out in time. If you are worried about fixtures being removed when they should be left, insist on an inspection immediately before completion.

Mechanics of exchange and the deposit

The exchange itself can all happen remotely. The rules are such now that you are not even required to sign the contract—your solicitor can do it for you if suitably authorised. Your part of the signed contract will then be sent off together with a cheque for 10 per cent (normally) of the purchase price which the solicitors for the seller will hold on behalf of the seller pending completion.

By all means try to negotiate on the deposit. Five per cent, 1 per cent or even a nominal £1 may be acceptable to the seller who is just relieved to get you on the line.

After exchange, the excitement should die down. Relax. Open that champagne.

COMPLETION—THE CONVEYANCE WITHOUT WHEELS

The seller gets the money, you get the property.

Completion is the formal act of conveying the interest in the property into your name, 'vesting' (the legal jargon) the property 'in' you. In practical terms it means the house is now yours, you get the keys, you can move in and you have a right to expect no one else to be there when you do, which is the 'vacant possession' lawyers talk about.

If you are the seller, do not let go of the keys before you hear from your solicitor that you have 'completed'. And as a general rule, never allow the buyer to occupy the property before the completion date—things could get complicated, however nice the buyer may seem, if the money is not forthcoming on the agreed completion date.

Completion date is fixed in the contract and it generally takes place 28 days after exchange, but it can be earlier or later, depending on the particular circumstances of the parties and where the commercial initiative lies.

FAILURE TO COMPLETE

Ideally completion should just 'happen' and a telephone call from your solicitor confirming that it has happened will be the extent of your concern. Sometimes, though, there is drama. This can occur where the buyer fails to come up with the money, or where the seller fails to complete because he or she (or his or her tenants) are still in occupation. Often failure to complete is 'technical', which usually means that there is a chain of transactions to be completed in one day. Unless they start early enough there may not be time for the last or later transactions to be completed before the banks close, so that the purchase money cannot change hands. Solicitors can usually agree some formula acceptable to the seller whereby the money can be held over until the next day, or the Monday if completion is on a Friday. But if not, the parties will have to wait 24 or 72 hours. Sellers can demand interest during this period.

If you as buyer cannot come up with the purchase price, the situation is more serious. The seller's solicitor will serve a 'Notice to Complete' on you. If you ignore this, and still do not complete, then you could lose your deposit (all the more reason for negotiating a sum lower than 10 per cent); pay interest on the unpaid amount at the rate fixed by the contract until you do complete (usually 4 per cent above an agreed base rate); and you could pay damages for any foreseeable loss that the seller might suffer as a direct result of your not completing. If you are in a chain and the fault for not completing on time is yours then you could wind up being liable for hotel bills up and down the line. Not a pleasant prospect.

There have been cases of sellers who are unwilling or unable to decant tenants out of the building by the agreed completion date.

In such a case demand all the rents that the seller received between the original date of completion and the actual (later) date on which you completed. If the money is not handed over, sue for it. You will win. The idea is that the seller holds all profits he makes out of the building on trust for you as buyer from the original date fixed for completion.

If either seller or buyer do not complete, the Notice to Complete is served normally giving a further 16 days to complete (unless modified). Make sure the notice is served without delay.

POST-COMPLETION EVENTS

If you are the seller, you take the money and run.

If you are the buyer, there are still things to be done, and, regrettably, costs to be incurred.

Make sure your solicitor applies to the Land Registry to have you registered as the new owner. The normal fee is on a sliding scale depending on how expensive the house is (e.g. £120 for a property worth between £50,000 and £60,000; £230 for one worth between £90,000 and £100,000 and ever onward and upward).

Stamp duty at one per cent is payable on the whole of any purchase price above £30,000, which in practice in the South of England means most properties nowadays. You have a month's grace in which to pay this before you incur a penalty fee, although no self-respecting solicitor will complete before getting the stamp duty in.

Apportionment becomes possible if the price of your property is around the £30,000 mark. Apportion part of the cost of the property to fixtures and fittings. This might bring the price below the £30,000 trigger so that no stamp duty would be payable and you will save yourself something over £300.

If you do this, watch out for the mortgage trap. Any percentage you knock off the price for fixtures and fittings will decrease the amount you will be able to raise by way of a mortgage so that the exercise can become counterproductive. If you were looking for a 100 per cent mortgage on a flat worth £31,500 (if such a thing could be found), and put £1501 down to fixtures and fittings, so taking the price below the stamp duty trigger, you could save £315, but you would have to raise an extra £1501 yourself.

The Scottish approach

Scottish conveyancing law and practice differs in important aspects, and the main points to watch out for are as follows:

• It is the rule rather than the exception for the seller to get the Scottish equivalent of the search organised. And this factor alone means that deals generally take place quicker north of the border.

• You cannot make your written offer (known as a missive of sale) 'subject to contract' because, quite simply, Scottish law regards your offer as the contract. Once delivered, acceptance is possible in writing by the seller. You can, however, make your offer conditional on anything else that takes your fancy (and which may be calculated to slow the proceedings down to a pace which suits you) such as getting a survey done, obviously mortgage finance, or on Dancing Brave winning the 2.30 at Sandown.

• You will be asked to pay a 10 per cent deposit—the full amount is payable on settlement (completion) which will take place on the Date of Entry (the day you take possession of the house) which itself will be set out in your missive of sale (offer).

• Finally, remember that the Scots have different words for everything. In addition to missive of sale, date of entry and settlement, attune your ears to things called dues (ground rents), and heritables which are what Scottish solicitors call houses.

3

GET SET—PLOYS, POSTURES AND TIPS

Remember, it is the house you are buying not the people that are in it. If they happen to be dressed in saffron robes, chanting mantras, and incense lingers in the woodwork, do not be either deterred from buying, or seduced into buying—depending on your tastes—on that account alone. Nevertheless, the vibes you pick up in the first five minutes are going to last you through what may turn out to be a tediously lengthy transaction. Allow for their effect on your judgement.

You don't have to be a walking negotiating machine for this game, but equally, complete innocence isn't so practical either. So pay attention to the following details.

Before you make an offer, or negotiate on a price once the offer has been made, you will need answers to a number of questions. You must get them in the right order.

Always find out

- How long the property has been on the market?

- How many other people have seen the property: are you the first or the 53rd?

- Have there been other offers? If so, what were they and why were they not accepted?

- If they were accepted why did the deal not go through?

- Has the house or flat been structurally surveyed? If so, did it pass or fail? If it failed, why?

- If a previous deal fell through, why did it fall through?
- Why is the seller selling?
- How long has the seller lived there?
- Has the seller found a place to live?

Memorise these questions and put them to the seller casually when you are walking round the place. Try to remember what is said. Do not make notes, it will not help the atmosphere. No need to be heavy about it, but get some answers.

Some of the answers will lead to other questions until the picture begins to build up of precisely how desirable the house or flat is, whether you have to move fast, whether you can negotiate, and, fundamentally, whether you want the place at all.

Points to remember

- You cannot place any legal reliance on the truth of the seller's answers—there will be a clause in the contract getting the seller off the hook from the consequences of any spoken words which may have passed between the two of you.

- If the house is described as 'fresh' or 'just' on the market, find out what that means. Some agents or sellers go in for the practice of 'bed and breakfasting' whereby properties that have been on the market for ages are taken off for a week or two, or over a weekend, so that the seller can in all good conscience claim that when the property comes back on the market it is 'just on the market'. This is a cosmetic ruse. Sometimes the real answer is that it is fresh on the market at a lower price, having been available at a higher price without offers for months.

- If you are the first person, or one of the first, to see the property you have the edge. If in your judgement the house is bound to go for the asking price or more, then you could deliver a knock-out blow of the asking price, but always on condition that the seller takes the house off the market and you proceed to an early exchange of contracts subject to search. You can chip away at the price once the competition is well out of the way and the seller, if the deal is to go through, has no alternative but to agree. The danger here is that the seller might have found it too easy to sell, the suggestion being that the house is underpriced. He may keep it on the market and attempt to gazump you.

- There are two questions which you must get in the right order:

First, has there been much interest in the house? The seller will want to say yes even if there has been no interest—you give him a chance to do so. Then ask, have there been any offers? If the answer is 'no', you know that people have been round, but no offers were made.

But if you first ask whether there have been any offers (answer 'no') and then ask whether many people have been round, you give the seller a let-out. With relief he can always say that there have been no offers because scarcely anyone has been round to see the house, which may not be true.

● Watch out for evasiveness on the question of previous offers which have been accepted but fallen through. The seller may try to disguise these by saying that the offers were made, but not accepted. Find out at what price the offers were made. The closer to the asking price the less likely it is that the offer was genuinely rejected. There will be some other reason, possibly sinister (failed structural survey), possibly not (flaky buyer).

● Sellers usually blame fall-throughs on buyers—'they didn't have the money'; 'they just decided for no good reason, not to'; 'the buyer was relocated to Hong Kong'; rarely will they come clean and talk about the reasons for the failed structural survey.

So give high marks for genuine openness in matters relating to the condition of the property. If the seller is honest about this, it is a good indication that he or she will be honest in other departments. It is a painful thing to be honest about. If the seller points to dry rot, take heart. Dry rot is curable, and this seller is likely to take it into account in the price.

● Get the seller to indemnify you for your expenses if the deal, through no fault of your own, does not go ahead. If you pull out or if the deal goes ahead and is finally completed then fine, you will pay your costs. But if for any reason the seller backs off (if he or she sells to someone else at a higher price, or if the seller's own purchase falls through and he cannot sell at all, or indeed for any reason that can be said to be his fault) he should pay your expenses.

If there is resistance to this perfectly reasonable idea, suggest a fixed figure—say £400—which would cover the mortgage valuation figure of around £300 and £100 of solicitor's expenses. Point out that really it makes sense. If you, the buyer, pull out, you pay; and if the seller, for example, decides to accept a higher offer then his loss is minimal and he or she still has your offer to fall back on if the subsequent deal does not go ahead (assuming you still want to do the deal). If this is not acceptable you will be 'worried' about the genuineness of their desire to do the deal. Particularly where there is a hint of a contract race, you should always demand an indemnity for expenses if ultimately you do not get the house.

- As a precaution against gazumping, indicate to the seller that you will be prepared to go for an early exchange, if it is in both your and the seller's interests. Do not fix a specific date (exchange always takes longer than you think and this could work against you) unless the seller really insists. Be vague but enthusiastic.

- If another offer has been accepted and *you* have the possibility of gazumping, the opposing offer has to be carefully considered. Within reason, and bearing in mind the state and value of the property, put as much distance as is commercially sensible between your offer and the opposing one.

There are certain proportions you should be mindful of. In a £50,000 purchase, £1000 might induce the seller to accept your higher offer. At around £60,000 you should be looking at a £2,000 margin, and from £80,000 up to around £100,000, a margin of £3000 plus is about right.

For some strange reason at around £100,000 people start thinking much more in fives. So up the bid by a straight £5000 if you want to knock earlier buyers off their perch at this level. Your aim is to attract the seller with a counter offer, and to deliver a knock-out blow to the rival buyer. Do not imagine that if you offer £500 more for a house worth £90,000 that the seller will be sufficiently impressed to do the dirty on the original buyer; or that the original buyers will not simply take this in their stride and offer either more money or immediate exchange at the original price. The idea is to make the seller an offer he or she cannot refuse both in terms of price and speed of exchange.

- Distrust sellers who are showing you around after accepting offers from other people: 'There is an offer on the property, but ...' They might let you gazump the buyer who is already in place, but they might, quite cynically, be using you to get a higher offer out of the original buyers, with whom they intend to do business all along. Be absolutely straight with them about this. Tell them you are not going to make an offer without a positive indication that if it is acceptable the seller will deal with you. Require the seller to get his solicitor to send out a contract to your solicitor. Check on this. Sometimes all the papers (answers to preliminary enquiries, copy of the search if available) except the draft contract are sent. The draft contract is vital. If it is absent this points to double dealing.

Reasons for sale

There is a reason for every sale, and it helps to know what it is. Don't necessarily believe every word you are told, however.

1 Developers are the most straightforward sellers to deal with. You know why they are selling without having to ask. They want to make as much money as they possibly can. It is a refreshingly candid approach.

2 It may be a forced sale—either as a result of divorce or lack of money—in which case bad news for them is good news for you. It suggests that in an ideal world they would not be selling at all. (Note: only suggests, you can never be entirely sure.)

3 A rather more neutral circumstance as far as the seller is concerned is where the move is forced for occupational reasons— a company relocation, for example. Again, reasonably comforting news for you, the buyer.

4 Sellers who sell through choice rather than necessity can usually afford to wait for the most attractive price unless, of course, they themselves are under quite separate pressure to act fast in buying the house they are moving to.

In this category, watch out for the middle-aged couple, the 'empty nesters', who decide to sell the family house once the children have grown up. They are selling because it would be more comfortable to do so, not because they really have to, and they may be difficult to dislodge except at a good price.

The same applies to people who are moving up in the world. Their motive is to reflect their enhanced status in life, and, if so, you can bet they will be straining as high as they can go, and will need every extra penny from the sale of the old place.

5 Sales for reasons of health are almost always spurious, and generally belie financial problems. The seller will say that either he, she or some relative is ill. Obviously a house with stairs is not suitable for wheelchairs, but generally no one who is happy in a place need leave it, even if they are seriously ill. Ask what the problem is, and judge for yourself. Do not be blinded with science. When you get home, check the story with a medical dictionary. Arthritis and back pain simply will not do, particularly if the seller is in a centrally-heated flat with no stairs.

Prepare to be misled If the seller has a story ready in advance, take care. That the question 'What shall I tell them if they ask why we are moving?' has had to be asked at all suggests that it involves an elaboration of the truth. Do not ask the question 'Why are you selling?' immediately. if the seller volunteers a reason for sale in a clumsy or inappropriate way, the odds are that it will be concocted. An over-elaborate reply, unusual reticence or blank refusal to answer the 'Why are you selling?' question, generally means financial problems. People will say anything except 'I need the money'. Of course if it is said this is music to your ears. The seller has given the game away, and is vulnerable to low offers.

Ask about the place the seller is going to—this is a good indicator of the reason for sale—the location of the new house and the sort of place it is. This may confirm or deny the story. For example, a desire to live in a warmer climate does not square with a move (temporary, of course, until we find something suitable in Provence) from North to South London. And 'Too many stairs in this place,' is fine provided the next place is a bungalow.

Where a seller has not found a place to live there are two answers: either the money is vital, in which case, fine, you can make a low offer; or there is something intrinsically unpleasant about living in the house, or in the area, which is sufficient to take the edge off life and force a quick move—anywhere. Watch out for railway lines at the bottom of the garden, or under it, flight paths into airports, traffic noise (double glazing on one side of the house?); and ask about burglaries. You may decide you can live with the problem the sellers are leaving, in which case, tell them that, you would, of course, be making a higher offer were it not for the fact that the Enfield Chapter of the Hell's Angels had its HQ next door. They will know the gaffe is blown, and in the absence of any other offers will be only too grateful to accept yours.

4

Go–
BUYING

Buying in a recession has never been easier, but it is vital to ensure that you buy well so that when you eventually sell, in whatever economic climate, the task will be easier. (For buyer's tips, see also page 15 of the Introduction and Chapter 1, Finding the Property.) In non-recessionary times, the first essential to keep in mind is that the dice are usually loaded in the seller's favour unless he or she panics, is badly advised, or must sell at any price. It is in the area of slow private deals rather than fast public ones (auctions) that the possibilities of real negotiation on price arise, but that does not mean that you cannot find good deals at auctions. There are several methods of buying, and you must know each well to get the best out of them. Here they are divided into five categories—some fast, some slow:

1. Auctions

2. Closed tender offers

3. Open tender offers

4. Fast private deals

5. Slow private deals

1. AUCTIONS

Auctions provide all the drama and excitement of doing anything fundamental in public. But the danger here is that you will go over the top and pay more than you need to. The trick is to decide how much the house is worth, then work out whether you can afford to go above that to make sure you get it. This extra amount is your reserve tank. Try to fix a limit. You will probably go over it— everyone does. But if you do, try not to go too far.

The trouble will not come from dealers. They go for properties with problems which they, with their expertise, can turn round at a profit—houses needing major refurbishment or houses with legal problems—sitting tenants who can be seduced into leaving by large cash payments after the place has been bought. Normally then, the dealer needs a 'margin', and if you are in competition with one you have an advantage. Assuming you buy the property to live in and not for immediate resale you should be able to bid higher than the dealer would be prepared to go. Dealers do not like sales well attended by private bidders. They stand in the aisles and shake their heads at the enormity of it all.

The problems may arise when you meet strong competition from a determined private bidder. There may be an element of 'auction house madness'. Auctioneers love this. The tension in the room rises palpably, and the result can be disaster for the winner, sighs of amazement all round, and a very happy seller.

You will be looking to buy a house with vacant possession or, at a pinch, with no more than one old lady in the basement. You will have to set up your finance well in advance. If you need a mortgage from a bank or building society, consult chapter 6 and apply for one. They will get the property surveyed and decide how much they will lend. You can then work out the top price you would be prepared to go to. This can be expensive: the survey costs around £300 a time and in the heat of the battle there is no guarantee that you will get the property you are after. If there is more than one property in the sale that you could go for, try to do a deal with your source of finance on the survey price (try two surveys for the price of one). Banks and building societies do not like lending on properties with sitting tenants, though they are prepared to coun- tenance a good deal of general disrepair. (Watch out for restrictions in your mortgage.)

Unless the place does not have all the usual guarantees (against woodworm, damp, dry rot, etc.—houses at auctions often do not) you should also consider getting the house surveyed privately— a structural survey. Here we can be talking £400 a time. A costly exercise which you may be tempted to ignore. If you do, remember that the rule at auction is *caveat emptor*—buyer beware—which means that you will be buying subject to all inherent defects in the property, pimples and all. If the property is tainted in some way, you can bet that the dealers will have seen it, and will be in there bidding against you. They will have a shrewd idea how much they need to spend and what the market resale value will be.

The cheapest solution to the problem is to get the opinion of the next best thing to a dealer—a local estate agent who knows his onions. What you want from him is a verbal assessment of the value of the property—'even if' it needed underpinning, rewiring, reroofing and had dry rot, what would the place be worth? How much would it then cost you to put it right?

All documents necessary for exchange of contracts will be capable of being inspected prior to the sale at the offices of the seller's solicitor. These include answers to preliminary enquiries on the Law Society's standard form, and a local land charges search of the property.

My God, what have you done?

Panic attack. Your bid was accepted and you have just had a property knocked down to you at auction. This brings in its train certain irreversible consequences. These are all contained in the 'Conditions of Sale', which you should know before you raise your hand, because there is no way of negotiating with the seller thereafter.

Once the hammer falls and your bid is accepted you are committed to the purchase. Generally, this means:

- 10 per cent of the purchase price is payable then and there;
- the balance is payable within 28 days;
- you have the responsibility to insure the building from that moment.

The fall of the hammer is really the equivalent of exchange of contracts in a privately negotiated sale. However, there are some quantitative differences. For example, interest rates payable on the purchase price for late completion are usually fixed at a higher rate than in a private sale.

'Unless sold before'

Some houses will be advertised for sale at auction on a particular date 'unless sold before'. Do your damnedest to fix a private deal beforehand and have the property taken out of the auction ('withdrawn'). You will be required to move fast, and to complete at least as soon as completion on the house if it sold at auction (usually within 28 days of the auction date), but there are two distinct advantages to this route.

First, you avoid the risk of losing the house in the heady and uncertain atmosphere of the auction room. Second, you might be able to get the house cheaper than at a well-fought auction price.

On the seller's side certainty of sale before the auction will be balanced against the price that could be made at public auction. Much depends on the property itself. If it is likely to be fought over, if people are going to flex their financial muscle and parade their commercial machismo over it, then the battle may be kept for the public arena. But if there is a hint of a possibility that it might not make its reserve, then a bird in the hand may suddenly seem very attractive to the seller.

Houses with vacant possession are generally kept back for auction on the grounds that they are properties most likely to raise 'silly' prices from the auction room floor. But you never know your luck. Make that offer before the sale.

How to behave

The ideal personality for the auction room is probably the sensibly determined introvert rather than the expansive extrovert. Generally speaking, just behave normally, and if you do not normally behave normally, then try to do so. Try not to drink before the sale—you might wind up paying too much.

There are apocryphal stories of bidders catching the eye of the auctioneer, raising their eyebrows and then discovering to general acclaim that they have just become the proud new owner of a row of semi-detached garages. This should never happen. You may see some dealers bidding with the merest movement of their index finger, but rest assured, the auctioneer knows them well, knows their habits, and knows what they are doing. If he does not know you, then attract his attention in a definite way, nothing too outlandish, try waving the catalogue. If he does not see you, call the bid out loud. If still no response, stand up, call out and wave the catalogue. It should work.

If you go to the auction with your husband or wife or a friend, stay together. And if you do get separated, DO NOT BID AGAINST EACH OTHER. It has been known.

2. CLOSED TENDER OFFERS

The difference here is that, unlike an auction which is public, closed tender offers are private. As at auction, the seller has created an environment where you have to play strictly according to a set of rules and terms which cannot be varied. You will be asked to submit a written offer in a sealed envelope to be delivered to the seller's agents by a particular date. The agent will open the letters and generally, though not always, the property goes to the highest bidder.

There again, all the documents necessary for you to see before exchange of contracts will be available (answers to preliminary enquiries, searches, documents of title) for you to inspect. Any additional terms (such as the interest rate for non-completion) will be set out, together with any restrictive covenants the seller wishes to impose.

This method of sale gives the whip hand entirely to the seller, and leaves no room for negotiation whatsoever. It is usually a requirement that a valid offer should be entirely unconditional (no good putting 'subject to contract' or 'subject to survey' on it). Acceptance by the seller of your offer may, if provided for, constitute a binding contract and you will usually be required to complete the purchase within 28 days.

If none of the offers comes up to the seller's expectations, the seller can reserve the right to refuse even the highest. And rules can be made up along the way, so that the seller could accept the offer he or she likes best, not necessarily the highest—this often happens where properties are sold for refurbishment, and where aesthetic judgment, or lack of it, is a factor.

Usually there is no chance of the buyer being able to purchase beforehand. Unlike an auction, where the seller is never entirely certain the price offered beforehand will be reached on the sale-room floor, there is absolutely nothing to be gained by the seller accepting an offer before the closing date.

In a closed tender you cannot hear what is being bid across the other side of the room. You are in a sense bidding against yourself, against the unknown. Just go ahead and stick the offer in along with the rest of the tenders, and hope for the best.

Only if you can persuade the seller that for some good reason you will be unable to put your offer in at the closing date, and that it *must* be considered beforehand, might there be some light under the door and possibility of negotiation. A convincing argument on these lines would be that you were going to spend your money elsewhere *before* the closing date for the tender offer.

Closed tender offers have none of the excitement and all of the drawbacks (plus some) of the auction, and are certainly no fun for the buyer who likes the thrust and parry of real negotiations.

Scottish deals

Unwary Sassenachs who set foot north of the border with a view to buying property should know that they are venturing deep into seller's territory, and it may well be Bannockburn all over again. The canny Scots have seen you coming and already institutionalised the closed tender offer as the preferred method of sale, particularly where there is more than one potential buyer around. Alternatively, if you are the only buyer you may be asked to complete the deal so quickly you will scarcely have time to draw breath. The procedure in Scotland (see page 32) has been finely honed in favour of speedy and/or seller-oriented 'closed tender' deals which leave the buyer the minimum of scope for negotiation. You can expect the seller's solicitor to behave with calculating decorum and to be silent on the question of whether there are other offers around, let alone the level of those other offers (in fact their rules of conduct prevent their telling you). However, if you are a buyer it is still worth trying to knock the seller off his perch with an offer which you stipulate must be accepted before the closing date for the tender offer. And although you may get no joy from the seller's solicitor, badger the seller for any details of other offers that may have been received.

Quite apart from the shock of the seller-oriented environment, any newcomer to the Scottish scene may well be struck by the extent to which solicitors have a hand in marketing property. As well as combing estate agents' windows and private newspaper ads, you may well find yourself knocking at the door of a Solicitors' Property Centre, in which there will be displayed details of all property for sale in local solicitors' books. It resembles the continental practice of lawyers doubling as estate agents and it is now the case that solicitors south of the border are allowed, following the example of their Scottish colleagues, to offer property for sale directly to the public.

3. OPEN TENDER OFFERS

The open tender gives the buyer much more room for manoeuvre than the closed tender. 'Open' means that although offers will have to be in by a certain date, acceptance of an offer does not, in and of itself, constitute an immediate contract. So you can qualify your offer with the words 'subject to survey', or 'subject to planning permission', and indeed you would be wise to do so, so that you have room, once the offer is accepted in principle, to chip away at the price, improve terms and so on.

Closing dates are used in open tenders more as a date towards which all the minds of interested parties should be fixed. Acceptance of an offer does not immediately constitute a contract so, even after the closing date the seller can in theory do more or less what he or she likes.

This is the disadvantage of the open tender. After the grand opening of the letters, the sale proceeds along the same lines as any sale by private treaty, and can be subject to all its delays, pitfalls and uncertainties.

The ugly spectre of corruption

Tender offers are open to obvious abuse. Everything depends on the integrity of the person who opens the letters, and even if he or she is honest, what about the secretary, the office junior, are they above board? There is no doubt that agents have their favourites and particularly where properties are ripe for development. They have a curious habit of going the favourites' way. This is the property world's equivalent of insider trading, and if it is going on the ordinary punter stands very little chance.

But there is a way you can reduce the risk of this happening. Paranoid as ever, hand your offer in at the last minute, literally the last minute if possible. If the offer closes at noon, get the offer in at 11.55am and, if you can, hand it in yourself to the person responsible for opening the letters. Then wait for the result.

This reduces the time available for a bent agent to get his call through to his developer friend, and for the developer to rush round his amended, higher offer. You may be overtaken by a stampede of offers coming in by hand at one minute to twelve. This does not bode well for your chances and nor does it protect you from the agent who alters his friend's offer by hand within the closed confines of his office. But it reduces the odds against you.

What the agent cannot do, however, is ignore your offer if it is the highest.

4. FAST PRIVATE DEALS

Private deals can be the fastest of all if the parties are determined, the buyer has the money available, the seller has all the answers and a reasonably new search immediately to hand. A sale by 'private treaty' simply means a private sale, that is one that is not struck publicly, at auction.

The whole process, from the point that the offer is made through to completion, can happen in a day.

This is worth remembering when you hear the 'English System' being roundly criticised for its tedious slowness. It does not have to be that way if the buyer and seller are determined, well organised, and have their funds in place.

To set up a fast sale the seller should apply for the search well in advance. With search in hand the one real administrative obstacle is out of the way (see page 27 on searches). If planning permission is likely to feature as a condition this too is a matter which can be cleared in advance. The seller can get outline planning permission well before you even appear on the scene: it is quite legitimate to expect the buyer to convert the planning permission from outline to detail after purchase of the property.

Unless the seller takes the trouble to get these important administrative matters out of the way, he or she can hardly expect the buyer to perform quickly.

The 'deal in a day' scenario is really the hunting ground of the dealer and developer, who will have cash readily available, and amongst private punters, the rarest of all, the genuine cash buyer who can write out a cheque without needing to consult a bank or building society. The kinds of properties that change hands in very quick deals tend to come from different ends of the spectrum— unmortgageable properties for which cash must be paid (again, developers' territory) and top-end of the market, residential property where normal financial considerations just do not apply. Whether the threat of being gazumped is real or not, the speed of these deals reflects the buyer's paranoia that the worst might happen. Sometimes the deal happens so fast because the buyer is in fact doing the gazumping.

In order to be a player in this game, you have to have the necessary financial muscle, and, vitally, a solicitor who can devote all day, perhaps a night and the next day, to the cause. This kind of service does not come cheap.

For those who are quick on the draw

As a buyer who has sold you will have the added edge and security of knowing that you have flexibility and that you will never need to go cap in hand to the bank for an open-ended bridging loan of massive proportions. Instead the bank manager will give you an 'A' for living on your wits and initiative.

At the lower end of the market, the sellers will themselves be poorer, less flexible and well into the English frame of mind whereby (for very good reasons, as it turns out) you have to synchronise buying and selling. So if you, a cash rich 'already sold' buyer, swirl expansively into the front room of an £85,000 terraced house claiming the ability to do the deal within a week, the chances are that, even if you are believed, the seller will be quite unable and unwilling to move so fast.

The key to all this is to sell and sort out all your affairs well in advance—a rare and courageous decision in a country fascinated by chains and obsessed by synchronising purchase and sale.

5. SLOW PRIVATE DEALS

Time to face facts. Most of you are never going to get to travel on the super-highways of residential commerce, the auction, the tender offer and the fast private deal.

It is the lot of the vast majority to travel by necessity on the B roads. They are slow, there are hold-ups and jams all the time. They have hazards all of their own and there is absolutely no guarantee that they will get you to where you think you are going. You may very well have the interesting experience of winding up somewhere else entirely.

Chains

'I'm in a chain' people tell you. And now is your chance to find out what that apt description means in terms of pain. Most of you will have no choice but to synchronise your purchase with your sale. The person selling the house or flat you are moving to similarly has no choice; and nor, probably, will the person who is buying from you. What we have here, of course, is nothing less than ... A CHAIN—a series of related transactions, each being dependent on another, or a housing chain. The ugly situation arises whereby your fate is in the hands of others over whom you have no control; and it is small consolation to know that it is the same for everybody.

There are ways to break free of the shackles, but it is dangerous, rather like getting past the castle guards and leaping to freedom over a rising drawbridge. It involves obtaining an open-ended bridging loan from a bank manager, and if it goes wrong you will wish you were back in your dungeon, suspended safely from its ceiling.

Generally, if you find yourself in a chain with no way out, go with the general flow and hope that the chain eventually gets to wherever it is going, and that your purchase and sale will eventually take place almost simultaneously on the same day, along with an orgy of related transactions.

It may be easier said than done, but try not to get involved in chains which are quite clearly going to come apart. The problem is that even the most apparently strong chain is subject to inherent uncertainty. Sellers often just decide they do not want to sell, and buyers can be just plain fickle.

This apart, if you have a choice of whom to sell your house to, go (so the conventional wisdom says) for the first-time buyer if there is one about. An opposing view is that the first-time buyer can afford to be as choosy as he or she likes, and that it may be better to sell to a buyer who has more staying power, i.e. the commitment of having put their own house on the market. Eventually, though, there will be some property being palmed off to a first-time buyer: the New Blood of the market. If you are further up the chain (and your house is further up-market), try to make sure that the house or flat that is being sold, way down the chain, to the first-time buyer is reasonably saleable, and not a heap of rubbish with a council closing order on it. Ask all sorts of questions of the buyer of your property. If there are going to be problems they will appear in the lower reaches of the chain.

SPECIAL STATUS DEALS—ACORNS FROM WHICH FORTUNES GROW

The secret is that money can in fact grow on trees. Since the mid-60s successive governments have been anxious to promote home ownership, and there are various bits of legislation which give you the right to buy (compulsorily in some cases) the place you live in, or give you a protected status which you can use to your advantage in negotiating with a landlord.

Leasehold tenants with a right to buy

If you are the leasehold tenant of an entire dwelling house (a flat will *not* do), and if your lease, when it began life, was for a term of more than 21 years, you have the right to buy the freehold under the terms of the Leasehold Reform Act 1967.

If, along with your lease, you bought the previous leaseholder's rights under the Act then you can exercise your right to buy immediately. If not you will have to occupy the house for at least three years before you can buy the freehold.

If you are eligible, your first move is to serve your landlord with notice that you want to take up your rights under the Act and buy the freehold. Do not expect to be popular. 'Iniquitous' is one of the more printable adjectives landlords use to describe this particular piece of legislation. They hate it. In 1985, the country's biggest landlord, the Duke of Westminster, went so far as to challenge the Act's validity in the European Court of Human Rights. He lost.

Do not expect any co-operation at all from the freeholder. And also, do not expect him to give his interest away. There will be plenty of argy-bargy over the price, though you should take comfort from the fact that there exists a formula of truly evil complexity for working out the value of the freehold, and you may need a competent surveyor, not to mention a solicitor on your side to argue the point.

On the basis of the formula a property worth £100,000 in Inner London with 25 years to run on the lease would produce a value for the freehold in the £6,000-£8,000 range.

Cunning freeholders will say to hell with your fancy formula. They will be aware that unless you agree to their figure, the whole matter has to be referred to a body called the Lands Tribunal for arbitration, and while the eventual result might turn out in your favour there is an enormous 'hassle factor'. So even though you know the freehold is only worth £6,000-£8,000, it may be worthwhile agreeing to a figure of up to £12,000 for the sake of agreement and a speedy deal. The premium (the difference) will be the price you pay for a modicum of co-operation.

The deal will, in fact, proceed along normal lines for a private purchase, with preliminary enquiries proceeding to an exchange of contracts and eventual completion.

The net result, of course, is that you do very well indeed. The freehold price will be peanuts by comparison to the open-market value of the property with vacant possession. You can realise your profit immediately and move on if you like.

Buying out the freehold on a flat

This is not gold nugget territory but if you are a leasehold tenant it can pay to own the land on which you live, and not have to deal with tiresome, penny-pinching landlords who refuse to redecorate the hall in a passably tasteful colour, or at all, or to spend money replacing loose tiles on the roof. Of course, you would have to pay your share of the costs of this anyway, under the terms of the lease, but by buying the freehold you can see that the work gets done, and in certain circumstances this can increase the saleability of the flat.

You can either buy this alone (in which case you become the landlord and the other tenants will pay ground rent to you) or you can do it in conjunction with leasehold tenants in the other flats. In this case it is usual to form a company to acquire the freehold. Expect to pay the landlord up to ten times the total annual value of the ground rents involved. Thus, four flats at £75 a year would give a freehold value of around £3,000. Use a solicitor.

The Landlord and Tenant Act 1987 now requires freeholders to notify their tenants of a proposed sale of the freehold and to give them (collectively) the first refusal if they can match the other purchaser's offer. This involves a certain amount of hassle, but it could be worthwhile if it prevents the freehold from falling into the hands of another indifferent landlord. If you are only interested in a quick profit, forget it.

There are rumblings about possible legislation to force landlords to sell their freehold interests to tenants (rather than merely requiring them to give first refusal once a sale is on the cards), but specific details are difficult to come by, and no one has explained how common ownership of the freehold interest by the relevant tenants will solve the many and often intractable problems of leasehold living. As the lessee of the flat directly above you turns up the volume of his favourite heavy metal band at 3 am, will you settle back and comfort yourself in the knowledge that at least you are joint owners of the freehold? While the idea may be attractive in some respects, it presupposes that your fellow freehold owners will be compliant, reasonable people who will see things your way on every issue. Expect stiff opposition from many landlords, who tend to be influential on the conservative end of the political spectrum; and even if something does happen, don't expect that your problems as a leaseholder will simply evaporate.

Your rights as a sitting tenant

If you are paying rent regularly on a weekly or monthly basis you may be a sitting tenant under the Rent Act 1977. Unlike the leasehold tenant you have no statutory right to purchase the freehold, but your very presence, protected as it is by law, may be more than just an irritating obstacle to the landlord who wants to realise the full value of his property by selling it with vacant possession. Your 'hassle quotient' may be high, and two alternatives are available to you. You can negotiate with the landlord for outright ownership of the place you live in, or go for hard cash to get out—a 'leaving price'.

Your bargaining position will be much stronger if the landlord himself approaches you to see if you will take money to get out. The trick here is to get the landlord to make the first move. Or, put another way, if you make the first move you must do it in such a way that the landlord thinks he has made it. All depends on the art of conversation.

The preferred approach would be a throwaway remark to the effect that you could buy a place like this if you wanted to. Do not give the impression that the matter is urgent, that you have seriously considered it, or that you are doing anything other than making conversation. Let it sink in and see if he or she bites. By taking you seriously and coming back to you with an offer he or she will have opened negotiations.

If this does not work you will have to employ the direct approach. You will have given away the high ground (so that he can play hard to get) but it can still be effective and result in a deal if that is what the landlord is looking for.

When talking about price, remember this: some developers and dealers will pay up to 20 per cent of the value of the open market price of the property to get sitting tenants out and achieve vacant possession. Say, for example, the flat you rent would be worth £50,000 if you were not there and the landlord could sell. Start the bidding at £15,000 (to get out) or offer him £35,000 (£50,000 less £15,000) to buy the flat outright if that is what you have in mind. If you settle at £10,000 to leave, or agree to buy the place for £40,000 you will have done well. £5000 to go or £45,000 to buy would be reasonable and not to be sniffed at.

There is plenty of room for hard negotiating here, and you can instigate cooling off periods by just sitting where you are and not agreeing. Now that a fixed formula exists for council tenants to value their council flats or houses, a reasonably civilised thing to do would be to value the price of the place along the same criteria that apply to council tenants who are, after all, simply public as opposed to private sector tenants.

Where there is more than one sitting tenant, as in a multi-occupancy house, the situation is more difficult. The landlord may feel that the longer he waits for people to move on, the more money he will save. Elderly sitting tenants should watch out. If they show signs of infirmity the landlord may attempt to get them packed off to sheltered council accommodation on the grounds that they cannot look after themselves. But if the tenants are young and show no signs of leaving, the landlord has problems—even bigger ones if the tenants demonstrate a genuinely co-operative desire to be joint owners and appear to 'know their rights'. The landlord knows, or ought by now to know, that any attempt to evict you forcibly could propel him or her into the commodious accommodation of Wormwood Scrubs (or equivalent) via the Protection of Eviction Act 1977 (it is an imprisonable offence to evict or attempt to evict a sitting tenant by force).

Property for improvement

You may be renting a house or flat which, with money spent on it, could bring an even fatter return—a 'property for development'. The landlord may well be aware of this and so will be prepared to pay a higher leaving price or a smaller discount to the market value if you negotiate the purchase. It may be smarter to go for the purchase in these circumstances rather than take the leaving price. Weigh it up carefully. If you buy, you can carry out any of the improvements the landlord had in mind and corner the profit for yourself. You will be a developer, and why not? But if you decide to take the leaving price, make sure it is a good one. Say to the landlord, 'Look, I'm very well aware of what you will get on development. If I go you will have to pay me £X,000'. Go for a full 20 per cent of the market price of the property with vacant possession.

If you decide to buy, rather than accept a price, use a solicitor to front for you, if only as an indication that you are no pushover.

Council tenants and the right to buy

The great leap forward to a property owning democracy turned out to be tentative and, for most purchasers of unsaleable council property, a disastrous step backwards. If you do go in for this, be choosy. Remember that ownership brings with it responsibilities, and no longer can you rely on the Council's estates department to mend leaking pipes, repair roofs and remove infestations of cockroaches and Pharaoh ants.

Remember also that a flat on the twentieth floor of an otherwise solidly council-owned tower block is unlikely to be the investment of the century. Houses are a much better bet and the terms under which you can buy, although still generous by any standards, reflect this.

Flats After you have occupied the flat for two years you are entitled to a 44 per cent discount, rising by two per cent for each year of occupation up to a maximum of 70 per cent after 15 years. So if you have lived in a flat worth £40,000 for the maximum 15 year period your discount would be 70 per cent (£28,000) and you could buy the flat for £12,000. A very good deal. The ceiling on the total discount you can deduct on any one transaction is £35,000.

Houses You are entitled to a 32 per cent discount after two years' occupation, and the discount rises by 1 per cent a year thereafter up to a maximum of 60 per cent after 30 years. So if you have occupied a house worth £60,000 for the full 30 year period, you would be entitled to a discount of £36,000 which would be reduced by one thousand to the ceiling limit of £35,000 with the result that you could buy the property for £25,000. A give-away.

Restrictions on resale If you sell within three years from the time of purchase there are provisions requiring you to repay a proportion of the discount that has been given. Immediate resale will involve repayment of the total discount, and if you sell within the three year period you will have to repay an amount proportionate to the length of time until the three year period is up. So, if you bought the £60,000 house with full discount and sold it after two years you would have to pay back the council one third of the total discount of £35,000.

Financing Buying council property is essentially no different from any other private deal. Some councils will offer you a mortgage, but if not, go to a building society in the normal way, and organise the deal through a solicitor.

CHEAPER ALTERNATIVES AND NEW IDEAS

You can enter the property world by public transport with an assisted ticket.

Shared ownership and 'staircasing'

If you cannot afford to buy a place outright with a 100 per cent mortgage because the repayments would be too cripplingly high, there exists an interesting and relatively new alternative. You can both buy and rent. You buy part of a flat or house with a conventional mortgage through a building society and the remaining part will be bought by another institution (usually a housing association) to which you pay rent in the normal way.

The total amount repayable on a scheme of this sort (say 90 per cent mortgage and 10 per cent rent) actually works out cheaper than if you had to make repayments on a full 100 per cent mortgage, but it depends crucially on finding a building society which operates a shared ownership scheme with a housing association. These schemes are beginning to spring up in East London— pioneered by the Nationwide Building Society with the East London Housing Association.

Additionally you should ask the building society to arrange the mortgage so that monthly interest repayments are as low as possible, and this can be done by apportioning the mortgage between a traditional repayment mortgage and a much cheaper 'index-linked' mortgage which is adjusted regularly to take into account the prevailing inflation rate. You then pay a monthly amount in rent to the housing association to pay for the part of the house (say ten per cent) you did not buy. In effect you are sharing ownership with the housing association.

Let us say you see a house in a development which is covered by a 'shared ownership' scheme. The total cost is £40,000. You get a building society mortgage for 90 per cent of its value (£36,000) and the housing association stumps up the remaining £4000 (10 per cent) of the asking price. It should then be possible to apportion the mortgage of £36,000 between the repayment and 'index-linked' varieties, so that your total monthly mortgage repayments should not exceed £275. Add on to this a monthly rent to the housing association of around £20, and your total monthly costs are kept to a figure below £300 whereas, had you borrowed the full £40,000 on a 100 per cent straight repayment mortgage, you would be repaying closer to £400 a month.

You can then sit back and save the money you would have paid in mortgage repayments so that eventually, after two or three years, you should be able to buy out the Housing Association's share in your house—in the example given you would have to raise £4000. This is a process known as 'staircasing' and in this instance it would leave you with a mortgage of £36,000 on a property which is now entirely yours, and which may well have increased in value from the £40,000 which you (with your mortgage) and the housing association originally paid for it.

Consult the National Federation of Housing Associations for details of associations which operate share ownership schemes and the locations of the new developments on which they are prepared to become joint owners.

TIMESHARE—ALL THAT GLISTERS IS NOT GOLD

It may have seemed a good idea at the time but...Timeshares began to appear in the late 70s and early 80s: someone had the bright idea of selling 'weeks' in flats and houses, giving the timesharers the right to occupy the flat or house concerned for a specified period of time, rather than selling an entire unit outright.

The attraction of this from a marketing point of view is that you, the punter, are more likely to part company with a smallish sum of money, say from a few hundred pounds up to five thousand, than you would a larger sum. It is the territory of impulse purchases, hard-sell techniques and pathological salesmen.

Beware of anything that sounds suspiciously like a good deal, and of people who run public meetings to advertise and sell.

Timeshare accommodation is always located in traditional holiday areas and caters for the vacation market. So you can now buy yourself, if you so wish, anything from two weeks in a flat in Benidorm in January, to a month in a house in the Scottish Highlands in November.

Timeshare operators hold public meetings and push their wares with evangelistic fervour.

- Never go alone to one of these meetings.

- Never sign anything while you are there.

- Always take time to consider the deal and ignore any hard-sell inducements such as discounts for same day purchase.

There is no such thing as a genuine discount in a property sale. Ask yourself whether you really need a week in December in some windswept chalet in the Grampians, and are you going to want it in perpetuity? Is what was once a desire to go somewhere every year going to turn into an obligation and a drudge? And check out service charges—in all likelihood you will have no control over them and they may become excessive.

The timeshare market has, by and large, been a disappointment. The 'secondary market' for resale has in almost all cases, and certainly for timeshare deals in the UK, turned out to be weak. It is a very specialised market and one that may not grow into maturity. If you get tired of your week in paradise you will almost certainly need the help of the timeshare operators you bought it off—assuming the company is still going—and there is no guarantee you will even cover your initial outlay, let alone make a profit.

But if, finally, you must do a timeshare deal, check that you are buying an interest in a property rather than shares in a company which may go bankrupt. Your solicitor should be able to tell the difference.

5

GOING FURTHER– SELLING

You came, you saw, you liked, you bought. You even lived there long enough to get tired of it (usually seven years). You sat out the recession and now prices are moving forward. This is the time to get out while the going is good. But at nothing less than the highest possible selling price.

Many of the hints on the caddish and dastardly ways a seller can behave will be an open book to you now—unless you were already Streetwise you learnt them from the wrong side of the fence when you bought your property.

The Bad News is that there are no magic formulae that will make an entirely unsaleable house wholly saleable (and some houses will remain unsaleable in the best of markets); but the Good News is that there are sensible, streetwise steps you can take to increase the chances of success and to beat the competition. For tips on selling in a buyers' market, see page 14 of the Introduction. Above all, do not despair. Even in the depths of the recession every conveyancing solicitor has a story about the one that bucked the trend; the seller who gazumped while all the others were gazundered; or the contract race over the house in a street where nothing else would sell.

Seller's panic syndrome

The first rule of the streetwise seller is to avoid falling into the pathological frame of mind in which you think your property is worthless rubbish and that you should accept the first offer that lands on your doorstep.

In anything other than a buyers' market, never forget that your position as seller is fundamentally stronger than the buyer's, and though you can then go on to bungle the whole thing and lose the initiative, when negotiations begin you are always in the position of having won the toss. Even in the dire circumstances of a forced sale buyers cannot relax—while they may be getting the property cheap as a result of your misfortune, they are always looking over their shoulder for the gazumper, and they can never be certain that your luck will not change.

The manner of sale that you choose and the way you behave in negotiations will be influenced by the degree of your freedom to act. In the ideal circumstances you will be answerable to no one but yourself. There will be no pressing financial considerations, you will not need to move or be under any pressure to synchronise a sale with a purchase and, preferably, nor will you need to buy (you may already have a place to live and could be selling a second home). You have complete freedom to choose the method of sale, the price and the purchaser. There is no excuse for not having everything your way.

Ordinary mortals

Normally your freedom to act as seller will be partial only. While you would not mind renting or taking up residence in a caravan or mobile home you may have a family or children to think about, and selling before you buy may be difficult or financially unattractive. You will have no choice but to continue to own the roof over your head and synchronise your sale with the house or flat you are buying. You may well find yourself locked in the time-honoured chain, which limits your power and room for negotiation with your buyer.

Even if you are really down on your luck you should never allow a situation to develop where you need the buyer's money far more than the buyer needs your property. In dire straits foreclosure by a lender may be avoidable if you take the initiative to sell before the matter is taken out of your hands.

Timing

March to July is generally the best time to sell anything—whether privately or at auction. The market is generally slow in August, and while it picks up again in September through November, the deep winter months are also slow, particularly for country properties.

PREFERRED METHODS OF SALE

The aim is to give the buyer as little room to manoeuvre as possible. Auctions and closed tender offers (the equivalent of a private auction where you make the rules) prevent the buyer from negotiating at all. Of the two, a closed tender, run on your behalf by agents who know what they are doing, has to be by far the most unforgiving, ruthlessly effective and seller-oriented method of sale. All the pre-contractual matters are completed ahead of time, the buyer has no choice but to accept them and you take the highest price.

Remember, however, that auctions and closed tenders are often too hair-raising for the average buyer who may not, anyway, be able to participate because the timing will be wrong and there will be a need to synchronise a related sale. Depending on the type of property (the more up-market the property the more appropriate the auction and closed tender) the advice may be that a higher price would be available if the property was open to a wider public, although the price for this is that you will have to come down off your high horse and deal with the buyer as a fellow human being. You will have to price the property accurately, decide whether to use an agent or agents to sell on your behalf, and deal with the hurly-burly of offers as they come your way.

Pricing is a matter on which you should take advice from local agents whether or not you decide to use them to sell the property. You can confirm the agents' prices by checking comparables in the local and national papers.

AGENTS

When you appoint an agent it is fundamental that you ensure the agent works for you and is not 'turned' by the buyer. For much more on this, and advice on unacceptable practice by agents see Agents and double agents (page 116).

It is usually not possible to get one agent to produce more than one buyer for a property even where the offer is for any reason weak and the price low. Appoint several agents. Permit none of them to put up for sale signs until you have exchanged contracts (too many boards can give the game away). Try to agree fees of no more than 2 per cent plus VAT for multiple agency arrangements. And this should not stop you from tying up a private non-agency sale if it comes your way. Advertise locally (and nationally if the property is sufficiently interesting) either in tandem with or as a prelude to appointing agents.

Agents' particulars Where necessary edit these for untruths and overstatement. You will be wasting both your and the buyer's time if the property is not accurately and, within reason, honestly described, particularly in a recessionary market. Use plain English. Words like 'bijou' are unhelpful—if it means small, then say 'small'. 'Possible fifth bedroom' usually means boxroom or walk-in cupboard. 'Town garden' means room for dustbins and one chair or bicycle. If so, say so. People can usually see through agents' language, and it is better for the potential buyer to be pleasantly surprised rather than disappointed when the property does not match up to the fantasies encouraged by misleading particulars. You can even try leaving something off the particulars so that buyers can 'discover' it for themselves. If they feel the discovery is theirs it adds to their sense of excitement and can be responsible for that compulsive, pit of the stomach feeling that they 'must have' the property.

THE VISIT

Tidy the house, but if you are not a naturally tidy person do not turn the place into something that is foreign even to you and which may make you feel unrelaxed when you are showing potential buyers around.

Cleanliness is preferable to tidiness. Try to eradicate any un-pleasant smells, particularly in kitchen and bathroom. Seduce the visitors through the olfactory system (sense of smell). Coffee grounds are the obvious thing to be burning, though the Streetwise buyer will know what is going on. A more interesting and much less obvious method might be to spray the place with, if you can get them, natural pheromones or their derivatives, which are powerful sexual attractants. The visitor might not be able to leave without making an offer, either for you or, preferably, the house, and the visit might proceed like some charmed Pinter script, with a happy ending of course. At any rate it is a good excuse to wander round Soho in your search for the ultimate spray.

Behave as calmly, nonchalantly and unaggressively as you can. A good technique is to walk the visitor round the house or flat and then suggest that they take themselves round again if they feel like it. If they are interested they may do, if not they can make their excuses and go. It is generally not a good idea to try to make 'contact' with the visitor even if a handshake reveals you are both into freemasonry—it is the other sort of masonry you're trying to sell—unless it is a very natural outcome of your meeting, and not to go out of your way artificially to find things in common. As a defence against feeling threatened, some sellers react by becoming over-friendly, and this can detract from the visitors' appreciation of the house. If you do this they will feel crowded, want to get out, and may interpret your friendliness as desperation to sell so that a low offer will be acceptable. Nothing can kill a deal faster.

You may need practice, so try going round the house with a friend, or indeed, with no one at all, drawing the 'visitor's' attention to any points that ought not to be missed. It is not necessary to point out every electrical socket, but there is nothing wrong with stating the obvious (and anyway, depending on the house it may not be) so do not be afraid to say, 'This is the dining-room, and as you can see, there's a fireplace.' Leave them to ask the question 'Does the fireplace work?' They have to participate somehow.

If the bank is breathing down your neck and is poised to foreclose, or if you are being stretched to twice your normal length on the rack of an open-ended bridging loan, you are unlikely to be the most subtle communicator of the advantages of your property. If so, get someone else to do the showing round. Get the agent to earn some of the fee, though you should emphasise that not a word of your quandary should be breathed to potential buyer, on pain of immediate dismissal.

Hard Sell, Soft Sell, No Sell

The downbeat *Soft Sell* approach is to be preferred to the *Hard Sell* of aggressive marketing, which is usually inappropriate and may frighten quite reasonable buyers away. Some people have luck with a variety of the soft sell method, the even more laid back *No Sell* approach, where the seller appears fatalistic and depressed, even pointing out serious defects to the buyer. This has a curiously winning appeal, makes some potential buyers brim-full with en-thusiasm and optimism even to the point where they start to make excuses on your behalf. But be careful not to overdo the No Sell technique—it can easily backfire, because, of course, there are the beginnings of a paradox in the position of a seller who is selling his property but appears to be doing his best not to sell it. It may raise more questions than you would wish to answer.

Tell the truth, the whole truth, well, most of the truth

If you are a No Sell seller then you are going to be pathologically honest about all the drawbacks in the house. Otherwise, you can say what you like (your solicitor will include a clause in the contract absolving you from anything said in the course of a conversation). So you can tell the most fantastic whoppers without getting yourself into any legal trouble. The buyer cannot say after buying the house, 'But you said...'

Quite apart from the moral issue, it may, from a very practical standpoint, not be in your interest to lie. If the buyer discovers that you have lied about something (you swear that the place does not have woodworm, for example, and the buyer later finds that it does) it may undermine the credibility of anything else you have said which happens to be accurate and truthful. Cordial relations can be soured and deals can fall through as a result.

The answer is that you should be reasonably honest, which means that you do not have to own up to any defects or problems in the house that the buyer does not ask about. But do not attempt to deny the existence of the obvious. If you are asked about the bow in the flank wall, admit that it is there. If the buyer asks about the neighbours, give them an honest appraisal. If you have been burgled, say so (nowadays—the odds are that you will have been).

It is, of course, unlikely that a defect in any properly surveyed house is going to pass unnoticed and so the truth will usually out before exchange of contracts. You may find that a buyer will attempt to negotiate the price downwards if a defect is 'discovered' on the survey, but if you have already pointed it out, then you can say that it is nothing new, and that account has already been taken of it in the price.

There is one area where white lies are forgiven. You will be asked why you are selling, and traditionally nobody ever tells the whole story. If at all possible your answer should be of the 'not entirely suitable' variety and should be for reasons of suitability which are strictly personal, to you rather than the whole of mankind. Your circumstances have changed—you have just got married/divorced or have retired and need/do not need the extra space. Of course it may be that you cannot stand the traffic noise or the vandals who live next door, but obviously you should avoid mention of this.

If you are selling for financial reasons NEVER tell the buyer. It is an open invitation for the price to be talked down. Equally, if you have bought another place on an open-ended bridging loan and are desperate to sell your first place then for the same reasons

NEVER, but NEVER, tell the buyer. (See To bridge or not to bridge, page 90).

GRILLING THE BUYER: WELL DONE, MEDIUM AND UNDERDONE

You can have your buyer done well, *à point* as the French put it, or rare. Just as the buyer will want to decide whether to buy your house, you will need to decide whether to do business with the particular buyer, so the questions should be going both ways. In fact the bolder you are about enquiring into the buyer's background, the stronger the impression you will give that you are in control of the sales process and generally in command of your faculties. This will strengthen your position in any negotiations which follow.

Your interest in the buyer will focus on the issues of readiness to act and ability to pay. It is as well to have a checklist to make sure you cover every point. The buyer will fall into one of a number of categories.

The genuine cash buyer is a very rare bird indeed. This is the buyer who has sufficient cash resources to pay the purchase price without recourse to mortgage finance. They usually want to move quickly (very often because they have already sold their own place), but the drawback is that they are notoriously fickle. You might well find yourself falling in with their timetable, the danger being that if you do not, they could easily be seduced into buying something elsewhere. Make it clear that you are sticking to your timetable, and unless that is convenient for them, you should consider a buyer who is prepared to move (or perhaps has to move) more slowly. Although they have no need of a mortgage valuation survey, expect cash buyers to commission their own structural survey.

First-time buyers have problems of their own. Precisely because they have nothing to sell they can afford to flit around or pull out of deals if the mood takes them. Good, however, if you are going for relatively quick exchange of contracts. Always ask about the level of mortgage that the first-time buyer is going for—beware of buyers requiring 100 per cent mortgage—anything more than 85 per cent is a dangerously high level, and you do not want to pin your colours to the mast of a buyer who is stretched too far. Be quite straightforward in asking how much they intend to borrow.

Buyers with something to sell may have more complex problems. You will need details of the buyer's own house—where it is, what it consists of, whether it is being sold privately or through agents and, if so, which agents. You can then check with the buyer's agents about its saleability, but be careful what they say—agents are usually optimistic. (You can even make your own investigations— if the house/ flat is nearby (the average distance people move now is four miles) cruise past it and see whether you think it will be easy to sell.) Again, you will need full details of the buyer's financial position. As with first-time buyers, beware of high borrowers. If you are in the fortunate position of having competing buyers, you would favour the one who needed the lower mortgage.

If the buyer is in a chain make such enquiries as you can about the length of the chain. Your own house may be eminently saleable, so might the buyer's, but at the end of the chain there may be some trashy, unsaleable flat riddled with structural problems, and as a result the whole series of deals may be at risk. If there is a chain, or even if there is not, ask buyers whether, if the circumstances required, they would be prepared to bridge. Again, some say yes without really knowing what is entailed. But you can make your own assessment on the basis that the more the buyer proposes to borrow, the less is the likelihood that a bank will want to get involved in a bridging loan, or that the buyer will be able to support it.

Remember, the ideal buyer is not the cash buyer or the first-time buyer, but the buyer who has the commitment and financial stamina to run the course, as well as the ability to fit in with your plans.

SORTING OUT THE OFFERS

Competition is the key to the highest possible price and you should do your best to attract more than one offer. This, believe it or not, was possible though unusual even in the depths of the recession, and the evidence is that if a property is carefully marketed and sensibly priced, if, in short, it is going to sell, then you should be prepared to cope with more than one offer. Once you get more than one buyer interested you are in the enviable position of being able to run what is known as a Dutch auction which is a sort of informal, privately-run auction. There is nothing intrinsically immoral about a Dutch auction, any more than there is about a public auction— all you need are willing participants. You may impose a first past the post rule, or you may ask for best offers to be in by a particular time on a particular day, in which case you are running what amounts to an open tender offer. It is up to you to make up the rules. And, of course, you as seller can move the goal posts in the middle of the game if you so wish. If a better offer comes along after the auction is apparently over you can always elect to accept the better offer. Sharp practice but allowed. Most agents try to avoid getting involved in this because it winds their applicants up and it puts them to a lot of trouble, which, if their applicant does not win, will all have been for nothing. They would rather a cosy private deal be done at a lower price than get involved in the excitement of your auction. But in the end they will all play.

Essentially you can do what you like until contracts are exchanged and the game is over. Make the most of it.

Asking prices There is nothing sacred about an asking price. It is after all, only an arbitrary assessment of what you or the estate agent think you should be asking, and in market terms it is the buyer who establishes the value by paying the best price.

GAZUMPING

Gazumping is the practice, universally decried in the media and universally practised by anyone who has anything to do with property, whereby the seller, having accepted one offer goes on to accept a higher offer. The first buyer is allowed the pleasure of thinking the property is secured. Then comes disappointment. The shock is rather like being jilted and it must be said, however regrettably, that all is fair in love, war and buying and selling houses. Only a seriously deranged sadist actually enjoys gazumping. Yet it is all very easy to take a high and mighty attitude until in the heat of battle you are offered a clear five, seven or ten thousand pounds more than an offer you had 'accepted', but were not yet married to either legally or emotionally. If you are sensible you will tell yourself that it was clearly a mistake on your part to have accepted the earlier offer, because the market price turned out to be that much higher than you had thought, and, reluctantly of course, you will have to accept the higher offer. To complete the deal at the lower price amounts to giving tax-free money away to someone who in all likelihood will be a complete stranger and certainly not a deserving charity. Can you really afford to do so?

There are good reasons why you should always accept the highest offer. Assuming you have minimal shareholdings, no racehorses and do not own a collection of French Impressionists, your house will be your most important and valuable asset. Quite simply, you have a duty to yourself, if not to your family, to make the very most of that asset on sale. Certainly this duty overrides any moral obligations you may have towards a complete stranger.

Finally, remember that if you sold to the gazumped buyer, there is nothing to stop an immediate resale to take advantage of the margin you are choosing not to take up. It may be cynical but such things do happen.

There are gazumps and gazumps. In a sense a public or private (Dutch) auction is a series of little gazumps that happen so fast they are scarcely noticed. In these circumstances the players agree to be bound by the seller's rules and are prepared to fight it out with other interested parties to get what they want. It is not an activity for the fainthearted, but it was not meant to be.

However, even gazumping has its price, and practicalities do come into the issue. Suppose you are pens-poised to exchange contracts on your house at £90,000, the buyer has had the mortgage valuation survey done and has had the promise of finance, and all the pre-contractual legal formalities are out of the way. Then out of the blue you are offered £92,000. You would have no difficulty in turning it down, simply on the bird-in-the-hand principle. For a mere £2000 you are not going to wait around for a month until the new buyer is ready to exchange, during which time, of course, the deal could fall through. Furthermore, the value of any higher offer which takes time to come to fruition is eroded by the theoretical return you would have got if you invested the original buyer's money on deposit with a building society for that time. (So £90,000 on deposit at 10 per cent for a month is worth £750).

However, if the new offer was a full £5000 higher, then...who knows?

Gazumping without tears

The gazumps which are really going to hurt are those where you, the seller, have accepted a price from the buyer who has gone ahead in good faith and incurred expenses—perhaps a solicitor has been instructed, the building society/bank's survey may have been paid, and sometimes the buyer will have spent an additional £1,000 on a full structural survey. Then you accept a higher offer from another buyer with whom you eventually do the deal. You can expect recriminations, tears, even nasty phone calls and unpleasantness from the 'losing' estate agent (you may not be doing business with that firm again).

It is your job, therefore, to make sure the players have nothing to lose by participating (except the inevitable few nights' sleep and the lining of their stomachs) and you can do this simply by offering to reimburse the loser's reasonable expenses. That means covering the cost of the valuation survey and maybe throwing in another hundred towards the loser's solicitor's bill, if indeed any legal expenses have been incurred by that stage.

With expenses covered most buyers will play to win and that means good news for you both in terms of price and speed of exchange.

It occasionally happens that the winner of your private auction somehow falls at the last fence, has second thoughts, is forced to back out, or for any number of reasons does not exchange contracts. You then go back to the runners-up and offer the house to them at the best price they offered. If they refuse, then, legitimately, you should be able to withhold the expenses provided their acceptance was a condition of the deal.

THE CONTRACT DEADLINE

Use this to put pressure on a single buyer if it suits you and if you need to in order to keep to your timetable. But it is likely to be much less effective than when it is used to sort out more than one offer at the same or roughly the same price. This is the activity known as 'contract racing' and is an unashamed use of the system to your advantage, and can be employed as an additional and extremely effective lever in a Dutch auction.

Buyers, of course, hate being pushed around and while most will go along with a contract deadline if they alone are involved (hoping that the deadline will anyway be dashed on the rocks of their solicitor's inertia), many actually refuse to get involved in contract racing or, for that matter, Dutch auctions. Keep the players on the pitch by offering to pay their expenses. It should work.

GAZUNDERING

This is the practice whereby the buyer blackmails the seller into accepting a lower offer at a point when contracts are about to be exchanged. Often it is the result, genuinely, of valuers placing a lower value on the property, forcing the buyer to make up the purchase price from reduced mortgage finance. But where the buyer is simply being bloody minded, the situation may be easier to cope with than the low-valuation scenario. Be firm with the bloody-minded gazunderer. Wherever possible call their bluff; and if you can't be firm, negotiate. As with many disorders, prevention is better than cure. Try, try, even in the bleakest of climates, to get more than one buyer interested. And remember that the gazunderer will have incurred legal costs at the point where the gazunder is attempted. Small consolation, but it is at least some pressure in the other direction.

SLICK MOVES

- Very often the best way to negotiate is not to negotiate at all. The buyer may be surprised to begin with, and so might your agent, but once they get used to the idea, and provided you speak from a position of strength, it can be effective.

- Take the initiative—apply for a local land charges search as soon as you decide to sell, and do not wait for a buyer to come along before the wheels are set in motion. A search is valid for up to three months. A great time-saver, it gives the buyer that much less excuse for moving slowly.

- Always keep showing the property to more people unless the asking price, or something near it, is paid, and in order to achieve this expect to employ more than one agent.

- Unless absolutely necessary, do not get involved in conditional exchanges of contract, where there is any possibility that the buyer can pull out of the deal. You do not want to be tied down and unable to accept a better offer if one comes along. Absolutely out are contracts made subject to survey, or indeed any condition which involves the buyer's judgement, appreciation or reasonable satis-faction.

- Make a list of fixtures and fittings you are prepared to include in the sale. It saves argument later on.

- Get an indemnity from the buyer if you are asked to carry out any work at the pre-contractual stage—before contracts are ex-changed—and if these works are not things that you were intending to do anyway. The indemnity should consist of a promise to pay you for the cost of any work undertaken at the behest of the buyer whether or not contracts for the sale of the property are exchanged. Tell your solicitor to put the appropriate wording together.

● Involvement in chains of related transactions is extremely common and reduces your clout with your buyer. Pressure may come from either side—but you should be wary of employing the traditional solution—bridging—where you are forced to buy before you have completed your own sale. Much safer, if you can manage it, is to sell first, move into rented accommodation and then buy. Finally, if you are presented with a stark choice, you should bid farewell to the place you are buying rather than lose your own sale.

● 'Owner will finance' is an excellent way of facilitating a deal. It means what it says: you, the seller, finance the sale of your own property by lending the buyer the money to do it. Effectively this means that you forego an amount of the sale price and take out a mortgage on the property so that the buyer, the new owner, pays you interest on the loan. You can realise your capital if you so wish by selling the mortgage on to a financial institution. 'Owner will finance' deals are relatively uncommon in this country (but not in the US). And because of their rarity if you suggest this deal to anyone other than a sophisticated buyer, you will probably just get a blank stare, or worse, the buyer may think you are perpetrating some elaborate rip-off. But they can come in useful as a second mortgage top-up to the buyer's funds. You can set your own rate of interest (on the high side, therefore) and lay down your own rules of repayment. An interesting option for the financially-minded seller.

HOME IMPROVEMENTS TO ADD VALUE

If it would ever cross your mind to put a bow in your poodle's forelock then the home improvements you think up might actually reduce the value of your property. Some work, however, can be an enormous help towards increasing the value and saleability of your home, not to mention the comfort of living there before you do sell.

Windows The buyer's first view of your house will be from the street, and the detail which will fundamentally influence that crucial first impression, even if only unconsciously, will be the state and appearance of the windows. It is, as it were, a question of taste—better to have scuffed up Oxford caps than gleaming new brothel creepers. Best of all to have gleaming new Oxford caps. So if you have a house with old windows never rip them out unless you are replacing them with windows of the same basic design. It is a good rule for any change. You can employ specialist joiners to make windows to the old design, and there are plenty of places that sell sash windows. It will be worth the extra cost.

Double glazing This is an expense which can easily backfire, and the answer is, never do it unless you happen to live on a road where traffic noise is unbearable, or East Anglia, where you will be grateful for the slightest respite from the east winds from Siberia. It will cost £3000-£4000 to double-glaze the average three-bedroomed house and it is doubtful that you will see this back on the sale price. At best it can look neutral, and at worst very ugly.

Timber treatment and damp proofing More or less standard these days, and if your house has not had either then the reduction in value will far outweigh the cost of getting it done.

Central heating Becoming standard (66 per cent of UK households have central heating), so the same observation applies as for timber treatment and damp proofing. You will see your money back, plus more besides (the conventional wisdom is that it improves the value of a house by 5 per cent). Always go for the gas-fired variety, or, if you live in a place where there are no gas mains, get the oil-fired sort.

Patios and expensive gardens Taste is the key here, but do not get carried away. Any major outlay in the garden or around the house is not likely to enhance its value (bad news for landscape gardeners).

Swimming pools The luxury item of the 60s, the byword for class and sophistication, has, believe it or not, gone out of fashion, and any money spent in this direction will probably not be reflected in the price. At the lower end of the market, a large swimming pool which dominates a tiny suburban garden can actually detract from the price—it must bear some proportion to its surroundings. At the top end of the market, the discreet presence of a swimming pool—and a tennis court—is by no means yet standard, and can underpin a high price. But even at this level do not expect the price to be significantly improved.

Saunas and solariums Gimmicky and, like swimming pools, if tastelessly done can sweat pounds off the price of a house.

Pebble-dash and reconstituted stone facing There was a vogue for pebble-dash in the 30s and 40s and it can be said to be in keeping with that era, but any more recent pebble-dash or reconstituted stone facing work to a house can knock thousands off the price, so NEVER, EVER have it done yourself. There is no excuse for it unless it was done as some last-ditch attempt to hide a structural defect and, if this is so, that will tell you something about the house. There is nothing wrong with plain brick, and when it ages it can look extremely attractive. Where possible remove pebble-dash or stone facing. Rendering (the smoother version of pebble-dash) should also be removed, unless of course you live in a Georgian/early Victorian house in which case it is authentic, so keep it and redo if necessary.

Improved kitchens and bathrooms You will almost always recoup the expenditure in the sale price, though be careful not to go overboard with over-elaborate kitchen furniture. If you put a bidet into the bathroom, take the trouble to fit it correctly (*away* from the wall, you sit astride it with your knees facing the taps) which scarcely anyone ever does in this country.

MONEY

6

RAISING A MORTGAGE

Most of you will need to pay for your property by raising a mortgage. Here you have a choice between the devil and the deep blue sea: banks and building societies.

The Good News is that finding a mortgage is not like discovering the Holy Grail, and in due course you should be able to pick one off a rack while evening shopping at the supermarket. For the time being, however, you are restricted to banks and building societies who are falling over each other to offer money to almost anyone worthy of the title of wage earner.

The Bad News is that banks and building societies are parent figures of the most manipulative sort: depending on how good you are (i.e. how much you earn before tax) they will lend you money, sometimes too much for your own good and not without strings. They secure the loan by a charge on the house or flat you buy and are ungenerous enough to request you to pay the money back. And if you do not—on their terms—they can turn nasty and actually throw you out.

STARTING FROM SCRATCH

Let us assume the worst, that you have not even a bean to your name. You too can pull yourself up by your bootstraps and make the property racket work for you. There are two starting points.

Loans you might live to regret

You have no money in the bank, possibly not even a job. All is not lost if you have powers of persuasion, good contacts and plenty of effrontery. You will need more of this. There are fewer lenders about who will lend up to £30,000 and more for mortgages of up to 100 per cent without proof of earnings. Be careful here, not only may it involve you in making false statements on mortgage application forms but also, unless you are genuinely able to come up with the repayments, the whole idea could backfire badly and you could find your experience of property ownership brief and unpleasant.

Shared ownership could be the answer and you would do well to consult housing associations to see how they can help you and to find out where these schemes operate.

What are friends and relatives for?

It may be that you will need a cushion of a few thousand before you can do anything at all. So do a friend or relative a favour, and borrow the money, with a promise of resale of the house or flat within a specified time and in return for a percentage share of the profits.

It works like this. Your lender gives you, say, £5000 and you are then able to persuade a building society or bank to lend you 90 per cent of the value of a house/flat worth a total of £50,000 without any searching questions about your income. (The bigger the place you buy the better, because you can then rent out rooms to make the repayments.) As an added inducement, arrange for the loan to be secured by a 'charge on the property', which means that when it is sold the loan will be paid in full. Your solicitor will see to the details.

CHOOSING A BANK OR BUILDING SOCIETY

If a bank or building society seems to be offering you a good deal, it is not because they want to be nice or helpful but because they want your business and have to offer favourable terms to get it. Fortunately practices do differ and where mortgages are concerned you can choose your parents.

Rather than traipse the streets in search of the cheapest deal, your best and fastest bet is to engage the services of a genuinely independent mortgage broker (i.e. one who is not in cahoots with any particular lender), though guard against being sold useless life insurance policies from such people. Apart from the crucial matter of the lowest rate available, the broker should take into account other factors which will influence your decision to borrow from a bank rather than a building society, or vice versa.

Status enquiries

Any lender will want to make sure that you earn as much as you say you earn. If you are self-employed, get an accountant's letter or if you are employed be ready to produce PAYE payslips.

Generally banks are more ready to 'take a view' and bend the rules than building societies. If your relationship with your bank is good then the status enquiry will be a mere formality. If it is poor there will be a clattering of calculators and you might just be better off taking your chances elsewhere. In that case the status enquiry will take more time (up to a couple of weeks rather than 24 hours) but it may be worth waiting for.

Valuation surveys

Banks seem more impressed than building societies by the possibility of losing business because of slow surveying procedures, and are much more flexible in this area. They will arrange to have the survey carried out for you (average cost £300 plus VAT), but if you are in a hurry or can get the survey done cheaper, ask to arrange it yourself. They are generally happy to agree to this and provided the surveyor is reputable (i.e. sueable if anything goes wrong) he does not have to be on their list of local surveyors. This means, effectively, that same day surveys are a possibility—something entirely foreign to the much more slow-moving building societies.

Timing

It is wise to stitch your finance up before you even start looking for a place to live. Again, banks are more amenable than building societies in the sanctioning of loans 'in principle', that is, before you have found a place to which the mortgage can be formally attached. The 'in principle' offer will, of course, be dependent on the valuation survey and the sale of your own place (if you have one to sell). The 'in principle' offer should also be a bedrock of confidence in negotiations with a seller, and will enable you to say, if you have to, that your finance is lined up and that the survey, which can be disposed of quickly, is the only outstanding matter.

The accountant's letter

You may need one of these if you are self-employed or if your income derives from a number of sources. Somewhere in the letter the accountant will disclaim all responsibility and, having said that, should be prepared to say anything in your financial favour that can be even remotely justified. Lenders know that they cannot rely solely on the accountant's letter and that it must be treated simply as more evidence of their customer's financial profile. Providing it is favourable it should be sufficient to get you the mortgage offer you need.

If the mortgage application form requires you to submit, where necessary, your accounts for the past three years, and if you do not have any, simply append your accountant's letter. It should work.

Earnings multiples

Banks are less cautious than building societies, which is not, in fact, saying much. Although they do not like offering a mortgage of more than three times your gross income, they will do so if you seem dependable, are reasonably safely employed, and the property is problem-free.

At a stretch you can get up to $3\frac{1}{2}$ times income, and if your husband or wife happens to earn then that can also be taken into account. For example, if one of a married couple earns £12,000 a year, and the other, say, £10,000, then in these circumstances it would not be unreasonable to ask for a mortgage of £52,000 ($3\frac{1}{2}$ x 12 + 10).

Borrowing as a percentage of the value of your property

This is known as gearing. So that if you have a house worth £100,000 and a borrowing of £80,000, your gearing is 80 per cent.

The recession has reminded lenders of their corporate mortality—they are only as safe as houses—and the experience has traumatised them. The result is that their lending criteria are much tighter than in the boom years when 100 per cent mortgages were routinely offered, usually as a means of getting you through the swing doors. Many of them first time buyers, the recipients of generous boom-time mortgages are precisely the people who now find themselves with 'negative equity'. This is a sinister euphemism for the unfortunate position where, for example, a house worth £60,000 (having been worth £100,000) has a mortgage on it of £80,000, leaving the owner 'negatively geared' to the tune of 33 per cent.

You will be lucky nowadays to get a mortgage greater than two-thirds of the value of a property, and this factor alone will ensure that the recovery in prices will be a cautious and muted affair. And once the recovery gets underway, we can confidently expect the nice, understanding building societies (it's easy to be sympathetic when there's no alternative) to take advantage of an upswing in prices to foreclose on many of the dodgier and more dubious borrowers who presently 'possess' negative equity. There will be plenty of choice. There are 1.5 million of them (1993). The rule has to be: never borrow more than you absolutely need (not that you will be offered it anyway).

Speed cuts both ways

In dire circumstances you may be in more trouble if you borrow from a bank. Unlike a building society a bank will have its finger on the pulse of all your financial arrangements and will usually insist that repayments are made by straight transfer from your current account. If you have an overdraft they will usually see to it that this is secured by way of a second charge on your house. Whichever way you look at it, borrowing from a bank does not give you the marginal but sometimes vital flexibility of paying a building society by cheque on the day it suits you to make the payment. You can generally get away with late payments to a building society by up to three weeks. Indeed, if you start as you mean to go on, you can tell them in advance that you intend to pay for the previous month no later than the end of the third week in the next month.

Any further delays in payments will sound the alarm in the heavily computerised headquarters of the building society, and your name will pop up on the danger list. You will generally be notified by the lender that unless you respond to requests for repayment they will foreclose. The bank will tumble to your financial embarrassment much quicker and will have carpeted you long since. If the manager sees a shambling no-hoper in front of him he may well decide despite protestations that foreclosure is the only way.

So unless your bank is offering you a particularly good deal it may be wise not to let one hand know what the other is doing, and therefore keep mortgage and current account business well apart.

Arrangement fees, bank charges, complaints

An arrangement fee is a fee payable to a bank or building society for agreeing a mortgage or giving you a loan. Simply refuse to pay any fee for setting up a mortgage. Competition for business of this sort is quite fierce enough to give you the edge in any argument over whether or not it should be paid. Where loans (second charges) are concerned the position is more difficult. Banks often charge a half per cent of the total amount being borrowed and this you may not be able to resist, particularly if the loan is for some business venture where any risk is involved. If you refuse the bank could tell you to try getting the loan elsewhere, and it will be a matter for your judgment as to whether you call their bluff or accept the half per cent arrangement fee. As a matter of course, question all bank charges. They are notorious as being amongst the highest in the world.

All banks operate a complaints procedure and once you have exhausted this any complaints that are not resolved to your satisfaction by your bank you can take to the Banking Ombudsman, and hope that he can sort it out.

MANAGING A MORTGAGE

Interest rates

Mortgage interest rates fluctuate in response to changes in bank base rates, which in turn are affected by the country's economic performance, of which the clearest yardstick is the value of the pound in relation to other currencies.

You might think that if the mortgage rate goes down then your monthly interest repayments fall. But, depending on from whom you are borrowing, you could be wrong. Some lenders revise the repayments level annually, whereas others calculate the amount on a daily basis and react quickly to fluctuations in the rate so that the repayments fall immediately if the mortgage rate drops (or go up if it rises).

Although the amount you repay will eventually even out, it may be better for your cash flow to go for a mortgage that reacts quickly to changes. But be prepared to take the rough with the smooth. In fact most people prefer certainty and annual adjustments. Raise this with your mortgage broker to get the deal best suited to your needs.

In addition you may find that you have extra fees or percentages in certain circumstances. If so, threaten to take your business elsewhere.

● As the freehold owner of a house where you have the right to occupy less than 50 per cent of it. (You might sub-let, on a short or long lease, the greater part of it.) Building societies think this gives them the right to charge you an extra percentage on top of their normal interest charges, presumably because a freehold of this sort is more difficult to sell should they ever have to repossess. The arguments in their favour are weak, and you should resist any attempt to load you with an extra percentage. If they do not give way, take your business elsewhere. Remortgage.

• Where you borrow more than a certain amount, some building societies will routinely charge an extra percentage. For example, if you borrow £60,000, the first £30,000 will be subject to the ordinary rate, but the next £30,000 will attract an extra half per cent.

• Watch out for building society mortgages which charge a redemption fee if you pay the loan off before the end of the term (usually 25 years). Fewer and fewer do this now. It is entirely indefensible—the average mortgage in this country lasts for eight years before it is repaid by the sale of the house to which it is attached.

Interest relief

Make sure you fill out a MIRAS (Mortgage Interest Relief At Source) form so that the interest payments on the first £30,000 of your mortgage will be net of the standard rate of income tax. The bank or building society will see that the form gets to its destination, the Inland Revenue.

By using MIRAS you are having tax relief applied immediately to your interest payments rather than having to wait until the end of your tax year to receive a rebate from the Revenue. From a cash flow point of view, then, it seems very sensible.

Mortgage interest relief could eventually be phased out. So, if you are feeling cautious before you take on a mortgage, work out how much you would be paying without the interest relief. If you can only afford the mortgage with the relief, then, quite simply, you cannot afford the borrowing.

As with mortgages, lenders differ in the way they calculate interest relief. Banks tend to make immediate adjustments, and building societies as a rule favour the constant net repayment system which is worked out annually.

TYPES OF MORTGAGE

Endowment mortgages vs straight repayments

These are the two most common ways of repaying a mortgage and they operate in different ways. Depending on the level of the mortgage rate, one usually has an advantage over the other.

Endowment mortgages work on the basis that you pay your lender interest on the loan (this will vary depending on the mortgage rate at any one time), but the loan itself remains outstanding in its entirety for the full term of the mortgage. It is paid off at the end of that time by the tax-free proceeds of an insurance policy to which you have also been contributing on a monthly basis, and there may even be a surplus in the insurance fund so that you can not only pay off the mortgage, but have money to spare. In every month, then, you pay interest together with an insurance premium.

There have been problems. Holders of endowment mortgages are very much subject to the vagaries of the stock-market: things are fine when the market is on a steady uphill climb, but during the recession approximately 10 million mortgage holders have learnt to their cost that increased premiums will be needed to ensure that at the end of the term their principal is paid off. And not for nothing are 77 per cent of new mortgages of the endowment variety—it is an unpalatable fact that brokers and financial advisers earn large commissions from selling endowment policies (roughly equivalent to the first year's payments) and nothing from repayment mortgages.

Repayments mortgages are more complex and consist of a gradual repayment of the mortgage over the entire period, together with an amount of interest. The lender works out the amount payable so that theoretically, if the mortgage rate remained unchanged for the entire period, your monthly repayments would be exactly the same, even though their precise make-up would be a gradually shifting balance between interest and capital. In the early years interest would predominate and later on the balance shifts in favour of capital.

When interest rates rise you will find that you will be paying marginally more if you have an endowment mortgage than you would if you operated a repayments mortgage. This is because the increased interest payments are to some extent absorbed in the repayments mortgage simply by a shift in balance between capital and interest, whereas there exists no such safety valve in the endowment mortgage.

The crucial cut-off point comes when the mortgage rate is 11 per cent. On a loan of £30,000 over 25 years and assuming a monthly payment net of tax relief (at a basic rate of 29 per cent), you would pay £237 on an Endowment mortgage, and £238 on a Repayments mortgage. As soon as the rate hits 12 per cent, the advantage swings in favour of the repayments mortgage, admittedly only by £2 or £3 a month. At higher mortgage rates, say 15 per cent, the advantage is more marked still in favour of repayments—you could be saving a clear £10 a month.

The message seems to be that the higher the interest rate above 11 per cent, the more favourable is the repayments method. These differences are in fact magnified when larger loans are taken into consideration. Again, the repayments mortgage makes an adjustment between the ratio of capital and interest to cushion the blow. As a general rule, wherever interest comprises a larger part of the payments, the repayments mortgage is to be preferred.

Of course it will be the case that your lender will require you to take out an insurance policy even on a repayments policy—but this is to cover death only during the term of the mortgage and is considerably cheaper than building up an insurance endowment fund. On a repayments mortgage of £30,000 you might expect to pay insurance of around £10-£15 a month, while insurance on an Endowment mortgage for a similar amount would cost you around £70 a month (these amounts are included and are not additional to the monthly repayment figures given above).

If you borrow considerably in excess of £30,000 and if the climate is one of high interest rates, the message seems clear. Go for a repayments mortgage. If, however, interest rates are going to be on the lower end of the scale (say, below 11 per cent) and if you borrow only £30,000, then the Endowment mortgage is the one you are after. Let it not be forgotten that, at the end of the mortgage term, it is possible but by no means certain that the insurance fund under your Endowment policy may have increased beyond your or anybody's expectations.

Fancy mortgages

Fancy mortgages are beginning to be made available, particularly by foreign banks who want to muscle in on the lucrative mortgage market.

Fixed interest mortgages are dangerous for the lender but are available in various forms. Scout around and you might find a so-called **cap-and-collar** mortgage whereby you can fix the mortgage rate within a fluctuating band some way below the prevailing mortgage rate for the opening five years of the mortgage.

Also watch out for loans linked to money market rates (so-called LIBOR-linked loans) which are almost by definition lower than the prevailing mortgage rate. These are loss leaders, of course, designed to bring in high quality business and for the lender to make money on the later years of the loan.

At the time of writing the foreign banks, once generous lenders in the mortgage market, have disappeared. They will return—eventually.

Golden handcuffs

Some of you may be seduced by your employer offering you mortgage finance at a low rate of interest. Rates of 5 per cent are quite common and if you work in the City you can usually negotiate the amount you need. Be careful, however, not to overstretch yourself. If you or your job is ever considered surplus to requirements or should you want to leave the job you would have to move to a new employer who would be prepared to take on the mortgage at the 'soft loan' rate. If not you would have to brace yourself to the real world, and remortgage at the going commercial rate. The shock of this is something akin to a nose-dive into arctic waters; not for nothing are soft loans known as 'golden handcuffs'.

IF THINGS GET DESPERATE—DEFAULTING

There were 75,000 repossessions in 1992. Regrettably, as the market moves slowly from recession into recovery, there will still be a good many. When they perceive that the increased value of a property will cover the outstanding debt, we can confidently expect lenders to pull the plug on non-paying mortgagees.

At all costs you should try to retain the initiative. If you take action before the bank or building society are forced to do so, you could save yourself a lot of money, and you could save them a lot of trouble. This is an important consideration. Lenders do not like pulling the rug from under their borrowers' feet and will do so only as a last resort. It is bad publicity and goes against the co-operative, caring image they like to promote. Also, it involves a lot of hassle. And there have even been cases where they have been unable to repossess the house and sell it because the husband or wife of the borrower has had rights of occupation and cannot be dislodged. Bank managers are told that they have to get the signature of the husband or wife of the borrower where the borrower wants to charge the house to raise additional money. If they get this signature without fully explaining all the implications to the borrower's mate, any consent to the loan can be said to have been improperly obtained and the mate may well have continued rights of occupation even after the lender decides to pull the plug. The whole thing can get very messy.

You may therefore have three or four months before the axe falls in which to sort yourself out. You have a number of alternatives:

• For an additional premium it is possible to insure against failure to repay a mortgage. Examine these possibilities at the time you take the mortgage on. Beware inappropriate or useless insurance policies.

• You could remortgage. This means sweeping up all your outstanding debts into a new mortgage. If, however, you have been unable to meet repayments of the smaller mortgage it is highly unlikely that a remortgage will be the answer, or that your present lender would agree to it. Usually this route is only possible where you still have a job and if your house has gone up sufficiently in value to allow an extra borrowing. Go to a mortgage broker while you can still claim to be a borrower in reasonably good standing with your present lender and argue that you have run into 'short-term' debt problems, all of which can be solved by a sensible remortgage. If your lender has already started proceedings to foreclose, this route is immediately unavailable. And even at best, remortgaging usually only postpones the evil day.

• If you have been made redundant you will be trying, no doubt, to get another job. Any inkling of success in this direction should be immediately communicated to your bank manager or the building society. It can buy you more time.

• While redundant you can get the DSS to pay the interest on your mortgage, always assuming the house is reasonable for your needs. But watch out—the DSS may balk at paying premiums on life policies attached to endowment mortgages. If you can benefit under this system, check that it would be acceptable to your lender. Some are not willing to accept interest-only repayments and will expect an amount of capital repayments as well.

• Mortgage debts are generally the tip of a very unhealthy iceberg. You are likely to have an overdraft as well as debts to utilities (gas, electricity), rates arrears and telephone bills. It is usually possible to 're-schedule' these debts if you approach the debtor and explain the situation, and suggest that you repay at a fixed rate every month. Adopt a similar approach to credit card debts. You will find that the agencies concerned will be amenable to these ideas. It saves them the legal expense involved in taking you to court only to find that you are effectively penniless and will be unable to repay them anyway.

● If you flee the coop, don't imagine that you leave your debts behind you. Shoving the keys through the building society's letter box does not transfer ownership, and you will still be liable for any shortfall in repaying the mortgage when your property comes to be sold. This will become a personal debt and is one which will blight your creditworthiness for years to come even if it does not lead directly to bankruptcy. And watch out. If you rip out fixtures and fittings and sell off that expensive (and over-rated) German kitchen, the lenders will look to you for the cost of installing a new one if that is the only way to sell the property. Their arms are long. Their vengeance is total.

● Shrewd and streetwise to the last—you can turn the situation as far as possible to your advantage, and emerge from the problem if not smelling of roses, then not entirely without credit.

When it becomes clear that you simply cannot afford the repayments, take the initiative by informing the lender that you had decided, anyway, to sell the house. (By handling the sale yourself you are able to exercise maximum control over the sale price.) If you wait so long that the lender steps in and forecloses, you may find that they will accept the first offer to come along, however low, which is sufficient to cover the loan. This could be catastrophic for you and must be avoided. When they have a property to sell, lenders tend to send it to auction, pitching the reserve price at the amount needed to pay off the loan plus the expenses of sale. In theory you would get the surplus if there is any, but there may not be.

By taking matters into your own hands and controlling the sale yourself, you ensure that you get the maximum possible price. You can appoint agents or advertise the property privately. Alternatively, you could send the property to auction with a reserve price of your choosing, or operate a sale by closed tender.

The lender will be relieved to hear that you have decided to sell. If you are sensible about this and realistic about the sort of house you can afford to live in, there is every reason to expect that the lender will help you buy a new place with a smaller mortgage.

CHIPPING AWAY AT THE MORTGAGE—SHOULD YOU PAY IT OFF?

Apart from taking a well deserved round-the-world trip, this is what everyone who has known the drudgery of monthly repayments dreams they will do the day a sizeable cheque floats through the letterbox and lands on the hall carpet. A pools win, inheritance, tax-free pension sum—you now have the wherewithal to pay the mortgage off in one fell swoop. But should you do so?

Though it may help you feel more financially secure not to have a mortgage on the house (no more monthly repayments for a start), you may be able to make more money by investing your windfall and hanging on to the mortgage. The crucial factors here are the interest rate you are paying, the amount of the mortgage outstanding, the length of time you have been paying it, and your tax position—whether you are paying standard or higher rates of tax.

If you are paying tax at the basic rate then, taking into account tax relief on mortgage interest and assuming a mortgage rate of 12 per cent, the net rate you pay is 8.5 per cent. If you pay higher rates of tax then your position is even better—the net rate falls to 4.8 per cent at a tax rate of 60 per cent. If you can invest your money at a higher return than the net mortgage rate you are paying, it will pay you to keep the mortgage and invest the money.

Tax relief, of course, only applies to the first £30,000 of your mortgage so it probably makes sense, if you are borrowing more than that sum, to whittle it down to the £30,000 figure.

The situation is also complicated by what building societies call the gross annual percentage rate. If you are paying off your mortgage in the usual way at a more or less constant level of repayments, then the gross annual percentage rate of your repayments actually rises as the actual amount you owe reduces, so that if you borrowed £40,000 at an annual rate of 12 per cent, by the end of the 25 year term the gross rate of repayment would be well over 20 per cent. Obviously you are going to be hard pressed to find an investment which would surpass this rate of return and so, as a general rule, the longer you have been repaying your mortgage, particularly in the later years, the more it makes sense to get rid of the whole thing if you can.

If you do decide to clear the slate entirely watch out for the building societies' nasty habit of charging you interest until the end of the month in which you pay the loan off, and if necessary pay the sum out at the end of a month rather than at the beginning. And if you have an endowment mortgage (whereby a lump sum payment from an insurance policy pays off the mortgage at the end of the term) consider carefully whether you should keep the underlying insurance policy going. You would collect a smaller pay-out at the end of its term if you stopped paying the premiums (thus making it 'paid up') and it may anyway be a good idea to keep it on.

Once the full sum is repaid, make sure any 'charge' on the property is 'lifted', which means that the lender's interest will be crossed out on the register of title at the Land Registry. If you do other business with the lender—particularly if you have an overdraft with a bank—do not be taken in by the suggestion that the charge should be kept on to save you the trouble of re-registering it again if you want to borrow money for any other purpose. The real motive, regrettably, is not to save you trouble or the minimal registration fee of £15, but to secure the bank's interest if by any mischance you failed to pay off your overdraft. Insist that the charge be lifted, and if your bank manager then asks you to pay off your debt to the bank, you should respond in time-honoured style by taking your overdraft elsewhere.

Finally, you MUST remember to get new buildings insurance—the lender will almost certainly have insured the property, and on repayment it is your responsibility to do so.

7

BRIDGING

Forget gazumping and its cousin, gazundering—bridging is the stuff of real nightmares. Bridging is intimately bound up with the cut and thrust of buying a house, and can sometimes provide you with the most gruelling experience of the whole house-buying process.

Rarely do you start the whole process with the conscious intention of bridging. You find the house, agree the price, and everything proceeds smoothly. Then something unexpected and unpleasant happens. The seller of the house you want holds a gun to your head and says, for any number of reasons, 'Buy now, or lose the deal.'

In a buyers' market, tell him to get lost, and go elsewhere. In a sellers' market things are more complex but do the same if the circumstances permit. But if you insist on buying before you sell, and if the purchase is dependent on sale, then you will have to go to a bank and ask for a bridging loan. After the banks' experience of the recession, unless you fall into the category of 'blue chip' customer, you may have serious difficulties in finding one that will perform.

The 'bridge' refers to the time for which you will need the loan, which will be the distance between two dates, the date of completion of the purchase of your new house and the completion date of the one you are selling (which is, by definition, the later of the two). And the bridging loan itself covers this gap in time. It is intended to be a temporary device to give you the financial breathing space you need to complete the sale of the house you are selling.

There are two types of bridging loan, and they are as closely related as Jekyll and Hyde. The **closed bridge** is easy to get and almost a pleasure to live with. It poses little or no threat to you at all, and would be available in a situation where contracts for the sale of your present house and the purchase of the new one are exchanged at the same time, but the completion date for your purchase is earlier than the completion date of your sale. For instance, this might happen if the house you are buying needs extensive work done to it before you can move in. During the period of works you need somewhere to live, and why not stay where you are until everything is ready? Of course you will need to pay for the new house before funds are available from your sale, but at least you know you have a sale and you know when it will take place. The dates are fixed and you can make a precise calculation of what the loan will cost you. There is certainty all round.

By contrast, the **open-ended bridge** or **open-ender** is dangerously unpredictable. You may have your back to the wall for any of the following reasons:

● The seller of the house you want has been waiting interminably for you to organise the sale of your house so that you can buy his. But you have not found a buyer, or you have, but you are in a chain and the buyer of your house has problems over which you have no control. Finally your seller's patience gives out. Buy the house now, he says, or I will put it back on the market at a higher price.

● The seller already has a buyer, but has kept the house on the market. You arrived late on the scene, hoping to gazump the buyer who is already in place, either by offering a higher price or a quicker exchange or both. And the only way you can deliver is to buy the house without certainty of a sale of your own.

● You are the buyer being gazumped in the previous example. You retaliate and ward off the interloper by speeding up the purchase even though it means buying the house you want before you have sold your own.

In all these cases you need to exchange and fix a date for completion before you have done the same on the house you are selling. The loan you need to pay for the house you are buying is open-ended because you do not know when, or if, you can repay it. The date for completion is unfixed, unknown, and only on sale can you pay off the loan. Even then you run the risk of not being able to pay the loan off if you do not get the price you expect and need. It can be a hair-raising experience.

The mechanics of the bridging loan are common to both categories and are fairly straightforward. The bank pays off, or 'lifts', the mortgage on the property you are selling, thereby enabling you to get a mortgage advance on the new house from any source you please. Generally this will be a building society, although some banks may pounce on the opportunity for extra business and handle the whole transaction of mortgage/bridging loan as one in-house package. Try to resist this unless the terms are more favourable.

The bank will also provide the balance between the price of the new house and the amount you are obtaining by way of a mortgage on it. If the bank provides the mortgage as well as the loan it will be able to take a first legal charge on both properties, although in the case of a closed bridge it may not bother to go to the trouble. If you get a building society mortgage on the house you are buying, the bank will take a first legal charge on the house you are selling and a second legal charge (ranking after that of the building society which has the first) on the property you are buying. Whichever route it chooses, the bank could sell either or both of the houses to recoup the full extent of its loan if you defaulted and if it so wished.

Interest on the bridging loan will be fixed somewhere towards the higher end of normal commercial rates, say between 3 and 5 per cent per annum over the base rate, depending on your status. Usually, the more you earn the higher your bank manager's perception of your capacity to repay, and the lower your rate of interest will be. The poorer you are the more you have to pay. This is the way of the world.

To bridge or not to bridge?

The question will usually be answered for you at your first port of call by a figure as undramatic but vital to your interests as a bank manager.

If you find yourself traipsing from one bank to another in search of an open-ender, you might well ask yourself whether you ought to be bridging at all. Just because they are all saying no does not mean that they are all wrong. Bank managers are a predictable lot. If one will lend the chances are that most will. And if most will not, but you find one that will, you can expect to pay too high a price for the loan.

By differentiating between the non-starter and the perfectly reasonable request you can at least argue about the finer points, such as the interest rate, once the loan is sanctioned in principle.

Closed bridging loans come under the heading of entirely reasonable requests, are unobjectionable, routine, and should cause the bank few if any qualms. The risks associated with non-completion of sale are marginal and can be taken care of by effective legal action. No need to take any bullshit here. Go for a low rate of interest over base, say 3 per cent or even lower if your status is high. If they say no, change your bank.

Unfortunately the open-ender is by no means yours as of right. Too often has the manager seen his clients shuffle about in front of him, at a loss to explain why their sure-fire sale did not take place, and not for nothing does he now keep a box of Kleenex handy in the bottom drawer.

Unhappy clients do not contribute to profits the way happy ones do, and the bottom line for the manager who wants to keep his client is that in the end he may have no client at all. Open-ended bridging loans are always risky, never anxiety-free, and can wreck banker/client relations.

Even if you get the loan, do not expect too low a rate of interest, and do not be surprised if full structural surveys (costing around £300 each) are required to be carried out on both the house you are buying and the one you are selling. Any fundamental structural defects which may be revealed will scupper the deal (and would, incidentally, get you off a dangerous hook).

Now that you have got what you need, do you really want it?

Once you know what the terms are you should examine whether or not you really want it. He may have given you all the rope you need to make a good job of lynching yourself. Remember a few things.

REMEMBER that at best an open-ender, with all the angst and uncertainty that surround it, is guaranteed to take the edge off life for its duration. You are entering the hundred yard dash in the hope that it will not turn into the mile or, it must be said, the marathon.

REMEMBER, although your bank manager has calculated that your domestic income can bear the added burden of roughly doubled interest repayments, are you yet ready for such a brutal change in your regime? Or, if you are, is your family?

REMEMBER, if you console yourself that you are a high salary earner and that you have the financial stamina for what may turn out to be a long run, you will be making a big mistake. If you need a bridging loan you cannot afford to own two houses indefinitely. And the higher your salary the greater the sums involved are likely to be.

Ask yourself if you really need the new house. Is it so special? Are there others like it that you could buy at a more leisurely pace once your own sale was more secure?

If at the end of it all you are satisfied that you want to bridge, then by all means do so, but never forget (you will not) that unless you sell the house you are moving from, you may be going a bridge too far.

8

RENTING

NOT SO SAFE AS HOUSES

There are any number of doorstopping legal tomes covering the complex set of rules governing the relationship of 'Landlord and Tenant' as this weighty subject is known.

The fundamental danger for you as landlord is that you might inadvertently create a tenancy which falls within legislation protecting the tenant's right of occupation. If this happens the value of your asset will plummet—you will not be able to get rid of the pesky tenant and sell with vacant possession. The rule must be that you never enter into a landlord and tenant relationship casually. Take legal advice before you rent so much as a greenhouse out—it is no good going along to a solicitor after the damage has been done and attempting to untie the agreement. It just does not work.

The Rent Acts

These were passed in the 60s to protect tenants from the activities of unscrupulous landlords like the then notorious Mr Rachman (who more or less ran Notting Hill in those days). Suddenly the boot was on the other foot and the balance was redressed well in favour of the tenant. Landlords, who had never had it so good in the 50s, fled in the face of the Rent Act's two-pronged assault on high rents and unfair evictions. The important act now is the Rent Act 1977. It incorporates rent control, whereby a protected tenant can apply to a rent tribunal to assess a fair rent on the property, and protection from eviction, whereby unless a protected tenant puts a foot seriously wrong (by not paying the agreed or controlled rent) or decides to leave the rented accommodation anyway, the landlord may find it impossible to repossess the property and the tenant's occupation will be protected against all-comers.

Protected tenancies can even be inherited, so that when a protected tenant dies, a member of the family who shared the tenancy can take it on. When even this tenant dies yet another member of the family can, in the right circumstances, carry it on. It is sometimes possible for the landlord to regain possession if greater need can be shown than the tenant's. But this is impossible where the landlord owns another property, and is by no means a foregone conclusion even when the landlord is homeless (evicting the tenant might cause the tenant to be homeless). Tenants who have stopped paying rent can usually get a stay of execution for six weeks or so if they show hardship. Clearly the dice are loaded against the landlord, but add this to the time for bringing an action and if the tenant chose to defend it could easily last a year.

Protected tenancies apply to flats and houses with a rateable value of up to £1500 in London, £750 in the provinces, and because of the recent hike in prices in the London area renting a property even of the value of £150,000-£180,000 might be covered by the Rent Act unless the rateable value had been correspondingly lifted. It can confidently be said that any rent agreement that grants exclusive use of premises falling within the prescribed rateable band is likely to create a protected tenancy under the Rent Acts unless you have taken the trouble to create something else, like an assured shorthold tenancy.

OTHER TENANCIES

Shorthold tenancies

In 1981 the Government introduced the shorthold tenancy as a laxative for the relief of a thoroughly constipated rental sector. The idea was that landlords should once again be able to rent out property without the fear that they would be waving goodbye to it entirely. Shorthold tenancies were not covered by the Rent Acts, and any tenancies which were 'Rent Act' tenancies remained so, and the effect of the remedy was anything but dramatic, conspicuously failing to provide 'movement' in the rented sector.

The 1988 Housing Act brought in a completely new regime with two new types of tenancy, the assured tenancy and the assured shorthold (nothing to do with the previous and now obsolete shorthold, but the overlap of terminology was good for widespread confusion for a while). The assured tenancy allows the landlord to charge a proper market rent (i.e. no rent control), but the tenant basically has security of tenure.

The assured shorthold tenancy does not give the tenant security of tenure after the agreed letting period (which must be for at least six months), but the tenant may apply to the Rent Assessment Committee to fix a fair rent, whatever figure may have been put in the original agreement. Rent Assessment Committees are not related to the old rent tribunals and their valuations are meant to reflect the market rent, whatever that may be.

Before granting an assured shorthold tenancy, the landlord must give notice to the tenant in the prescribed form, otherwise he will not be able to remove the tenant when required. Therefore, if you are the landlord, make sure that the correct procedure is followed. A bit of timely professional advice (or thorough research) will save hassle and expense at a later stage.

Licence agreements

It had been thought that licence agreements were a way round the Rent Act. The agreement was based on the assumption that the landlord was actually living on the premises or did from time to time and that the licensees were renting only part of the premises and were not in full, exclusive occupation. But unless this is actually the case, the licensees (the people you rent your place out to) can say that the whole thing is a sham and claim protection under the Rent Act. Dangerous territory, and to be avoided particularly if you are dealing with tenants who know the first thing about their rights. So avoid licence agreements and go for shorthold tenancy instead.

Ploys

Where any rented accommodation includes the supply of food or meals, the tenancy is not protected under the Rent Act. So long-term bed and breakfast accommodation falls outside the Act.

Where rent includes payment for services such as cleaning, or ironing, there can be no protected tenancy. Service flats therefore escape the Act's clutches.

Lodgers

If you rent out rooms in a house which you genuinely live in, then there is no need to enter into any kind of formal agreement with your lodgers, or more accurately, licensees. The relationship is not covered by the Rent Act, and can be entirely informal. You can impose any terms you like, and ask them to leave whenever you want them to go. A useful arrangement for people who need contributions to pay the mortgage.

Holiday lets

Another way round the dreaded Rent Act is to claim that the tenancy is a holiday let for which the full protection of the Rent Act would be inappropriate.

In order to qualify, the premises have to be rented for *less* than 31 consecutive days by the same tenant and must be furnished; they must also be on offer for at least 140 days a year and let for at least 70.

RENTING AS AN INVESTMENT

Even assuming you are able to charge a rent which is not controlled by the Rent Act, and the tenancy is such that you can repossess without problems, there are still two good reasons why in purely investment terms renting a property is not a good way of making regular money.

First, the sort of rent you should be able to charge for a property ought to cover what it would cost you if you had to borrow all the money to buy it. For instance, if you bought a flat worth £60,000 and borrowed all the money to do it, you might be paying interest on your loan of anywhere between £7,000-£10,000 a year, or between £600 and around £800 per month. But the very most the market would bear if you rented the property out might be £400 a month. You are therefore relying on inflation and the annual increase in property prices to fill in the gap and make owning the property worthwhile.

Second, quite simply, you have to pay tax on any rents received, which is quite normal of course, but it increases even further the gap between the net rents receivable and the amount which, if you borrowed all the money to buy the place, it is costing you to own it.

You are never going to get rich off rents, and for most of you who become landlords renting will be no more than a sensible and convenient way of keeping your asset ticking over while the real business of making money is done by massive increases (if they occur) in the capital value of the property.

RENTING AS AN ALTERNATIVE
TO OWNERSHIP

A great idea while prices are falling, but when you find yourself paying as much in rent as you would if you borrowed money to buy the place you're renting, this is the green light to get back into the market as an owner-occupier. The point at which statisticians predict the market will turn is when base lending rates reach a level of 6.5 per cent.

9

TAX

RENTS

Any profits from rents you receive will be added to any other income you have and taxed as income tax. Now be good, and pay your taxes, and do not be seduced by riches (it is usually not much anyway). Render unto Caesar the things that are Caesar's.

What you can of course do is deduct all reasonable expenses from any rents you receive. Apart from rates and the costs of maintenance and repairs, if you employ an agent or property manager to look after the place on your behalf, these fees will be a legitimate deduction.

Of greater concern to you than tax loopholes (which can easily be turned into nooses) will be the security of your investment.

PROFITS ON SALE

Unless you are a property dealer (in which case your profits will be assessable as income) any profit you make when you sell the house will be liable to Capital Gains Tax with the important proviso that if the house you sell is your principal private residence any profit you make is TAX FREE. This is one of nature's little bounties, and it is important that you be aware of how it can be used.

Principal Private Residence

Principal Private Residence (PPR) usually means what it says and it will be quite obvious, particularly if you own no other property, that your principal private residence is the place which you own and live in. People move an average of three or four times in their lives, and each time the profit made from the sale of their PPR will be used to finance the purchase of a more expensive house, which will then become their new PPR. If they do so at all, it is usually only towards the end of their days that people decide to realise a little of their profits by selling an expensive house, buying a more modest retirement home, and realising some tax-free cash.

The PPR exemption is not an over-generous gesture on the part of the Revenue. They know that eventually they will be in for a piece of the action in the form of Inheritance Tax which hits the transfer of property to anyone other than the spouse of the owner during life or on death. But when the surviving spouse dies, the Inland Revenue close in for a handsome kill, so to speak, and the ultimate fruits of all those tax exempt moves will be whacked heavily. In this connection, it is wise for a married couple to make wills in such a way that on the death of the first of the pair the maximum tax-exempt amount under inheritance taxation (£90,000) goes directly to any children or heirs, so that the survivor's estate, which will eventually be hit, will not be ravaged to quite the same degree.

Making an election

No, you are not being asked to choose the next government. It may be that you have more than one house in which case you will have to decide (elect) which property you wish to be your PPR. No doubt you will choose the more valuable of the two (if there is a difference between the two). There are difficulties in changing your PPR from one property you own to another in the absence of some sort of proof that the move is genuine. You may start out life with a country cottage and then acquire a flat in a city. The cottage may be worth far less than the flat and increase in value at a slower rate, so obviously it would be to your advantage to switch the PPR tag for Inland Revenue purposes over to the city flat in which you might spend, say, only two nights a week. The best advice is to get yourself a good accountant and brazen it out. It may even be worth moving entirely to the flat for a while and renting the cottage out as if to underscore the authenticity of the whole deal.

The two PPRs gambit

The Inland Revenue are not entirely unreasonable and they do understand that there may be a gap between buying a new place and selling your old one. In the time it takes you to sell the old one you effectively have two principal private residences. This can work to your advantage if you can afford to buy without selling immediately, and waiting for a while (perhaps renting out on a safe shorthold tenancy) before selling in much improved market conditions and still using the PPR exemption to avoid paying CGT on your profits on sale. There is no hard and fast rule on this but the Revenue will, depending on your circumstances, let you have two PPRs for up to two years, usually not longer, and possibly for a shorter period. But at some point you will be forced to take the decision to sell one of the houses you own, or to keep both and 'elect' one to be your PPR, while the other loses that status and the tax advantages that go with it. This is what is known as an '*embarras de richesses*'.

Splitting your PPR into flats

Let us say the house proved too big for your needs or is too expensive to run, or you bought it with the express intention of doing a bit of amateur developing and turning it into flats. People are doing this more and more, but, quite apart from the fundamental economies of turning your large principal private residence into a number of flats, there are tax implications and the figures may not make the project worthwhile.

Of course, other considerations may put a different colouring on things, but margins can be slim and if you do not sell the flats at the price you hope for you could find that the deal will be at best financially neutral or that you will even lose money. Unless the deal is one that a developer would consider a 'goer' (i.e. one where you make at least a clear 20 per cent return on capital including any money borrowed), consider carefully whether you should go ahead.

Multiple moves: how long can you get away with it?

The principal private residence card is wide open to abuse or, depending on which way you look at it, over-use. Clearly the system was not designed to benefit people who make it their business to move frequently from one development property to another, doing them up, living in them, and selling them as they go along, all under the tax-free umbrella of the principal private residence, but if the Revenue gives you an inch, you are going to take a mile. The Revenue are not entirely intolerant of the over-used PPR card (there are much higher priorities on the list of people to 'get') and will generally allow multiple moves, say, six times in as many years before they get suspicious and begin asking questions to see whether they have a covert developer on their hands. There have been some really gross cases—fifteen moves in ten years with the average stay in the principal private residence of around eight months—and in these cases the Revenue commonly come to an arrangement with the wealthy vagrant and the usual deal is an allowance of say six to nine moves under the PPR umbrella, and income tax on profits from the rest.

It is all a question of proportion and the dividing line between a healthy acceptable number of tax-free moves and the point where it becomes a taxable business will vary from individual to individual. Some of the cleverest exponents of this art have been lawyers—solicitors and barristers—whose day-to-day activities have nicely screened the real source of their eventual wealth—frequent and timely moves up the housing ladder. You will arouse less suspicion and notch up more tax-free moves if you move from house to house, selling each house intact and without succumbing to the temptation of splitting the place into flats, which is deep developer's territory and a dead giveaway. In any case, the PPR exemption would only be of marginal assistance to you if you moved from flat development to flat development, retaining a unit for yourself on each occasion.

Of course it may just be that you move frequently for entirely innocent motives, discovering an intolerable drawback about each place you move to and inadvertently making a fortune on the way. Unlikely, but possible, and it is up to you to present a plausible explanation to the Revenue if you are put to the test. There is really no limit to the reasons for a move if you are the sensitive type—traffic noise and awful neighbours will do fine. A burglary can always come in handy if you feel your 'home' has been 'violated' and you no longer want it. So can doctors' and psychiatrists' letters. Remember that the Revenue are only interested in cases of gross and obvious abuse, so provided you do not overgild the lily by a truly staggering number of moves in a short time you should be okay.

MORTGAGE INTEREST RELIEF

For many people, particularly first-time buyers, tax relief on mortgage interest payments are a vital calculation of whether a property is affordable or not. Tax relief on a £30,000 mortgage (the upper limit of the amount for which relief can be claimed) amounts to a very useful £1000 or so a year, and can, in cash flow terms, turn a £300 a month repayment into a much more manageable £220.

Mortgage interest relief is not actually A Good Thing, because it has the effect of seducing large numbers of mainly young, mainly first-time, buyers into taking on debts which they cannot really afford. It also stimulates demand and drives prices up, which in turn benefits the building industry, which is thereby unfairly favoured by comparison to other needy industrial sectors.

What the government would probably like to do would be to knock mortgage interest relief on the head altogether, but to do that would cause a convulsion of outrage amongst the property-owning classes which would make the events leading up to the Russian Revolution look mild by comparison. But while it would be a brave government that would phase out mortgage interest relief altogether, do not expect the relief threshold to be raised from the present £30,000 limit.

STAMP DUTY

The revenue imposes a tax of 1 per cent on sales of all houses exceeding a value of £30,000. No allowance is made for the first £30,000—the tax simply hits the total amount above that figure.

HOME IMPROVEMENT LOANS

Interest payments on home improvement loans qualify for tax relief provided that the amount of the loan in addition to any mortgage you may have does not exceed a total of £30,000, which is the overall ceiling for tax relief on mortgage interest. So if you borrowed £15,000 to carry out some improvement, and you already had a mortgage of £20,000, then only the interest repayments on the first £10,000 of the improvement loan would qualify for tax relief.

The word 'improvement' as defined by the Inland Revenue covers more or less anything you might want to do to your home. Any major work of reconstruction and anything to do with sanitation (connection to mains drainage or the provision of bathrooms and showers) is covered. Surprisingly, so are a number of items that most people would consider entirely optional, or not necessarily an improvement at all. So you can get interest relief on loans for the installation or building of saunas and swimming pools, landscaped gardens, double glazing, solar heating and loft conversions, as well as more obvious items such as central heating and insulation.

If in doubt about whether the loan for your proposed improvement qualifies for interest relief, call your local Inland Revenue office and they should be able to tell you immediately.

COUNCIL TAX

Do the words 'Poll Tax' ring any bells? It was the aberration which came after General Rates and before Council Tax, the government's latest foray into the no-win area of local taxation. The Council Tax system is based on land values and no doubt it will work by valuing houses at prices they could not fetch on the open market, and taxing them according. Pity the South East and expect to hear much squealing from Conservative MPs. Doubtless, too, the tax will have to be paid under threat of a fine and/or imprisonment (for a short period). The government may also be expected to go in for rate-capping local authorities which it thinks are spending too much. Never before have local authority finances come under such scrutiny from Whitehall. So far, big surprise, the quality of life of the citizenry has not noticeably improved as a result of it.

The average Council Tax for 1993 is as follows:

Average English Council Tax for 1993			
Band	**% of properties**	**Illustrative 1991 Bill £**	**1993 £**
Band A 0-£40,000	26.3	266	329
Band B £40,000-£52,000	19.1	311	384
Band C £52,000-£68,000	21.8	355	439
Band D £68,000-£88,000	14.5	400	494
Band E £88,000-£120,000	9.0	488	604
Band F £120,000-£160,000	4.9	577	713
Band G £160,000-£320,000	3.7	666	823
Band H £320,000-plus	0.6	800	988

The tax may be higher in some places as a result of the failure of local authorities to collect Poll Tax. But there will be exemptions for those households on income support (numbering approximately 3 million) and discounts for single person households.

PROFESSIONALS, BUILDERS AND BUREAUCRATS

10

LAWYERS AND OTHER CONVEYANCERS

Conveyancing is a dark and lonely business, but someone has to do it. Unless you are a DIY fanatic the obvious answer is to employ a professional.

We know professionals do very little. But for those of us who are inclined to do even less, or who have better things to do (such as getting the highest possible price for our property), it makes sense to hire them, and to prod them from time to time by telephone to make sure they come to life and do something to justify their fee.

SOLICITORS

Solicitors regularly write books about their own profession which blow the gaffe and tell us how little they actually do. So now that their cover is well and truly blown, it should be possible to work on a solicitor to the extent that the fee at the end of the day is quite genuinely small compensation for the ordeal of having you as his client. When sweat breaks out on your solicitor's brow at the very mention of your name, you know you are through the defences and well inside the perimeter. Indeed you may be in danger of getting value for money. Do not feel sorry for them, no one has to be a solicitor.

Read this section in conjunction with the chapter on legalities (page 24) so that you know vaguely what ought to be going on, and, crucially, so that you can ask your solicitor apparently well-informed and maybe embarrassing questions.

Ideally you will be treated as the only client—though if this actually turned out to be the case you would have grave doubts about the competence of your chosen adviser. Be reasonable about the demands you make and, remember, that the more you pay the better the service you have a right to expect.

Telephone manners are a useful indicator of the kind of service you are getting. If your calls are not returned, or if the solicitor is always in a meeting, then you might remind whoever it is you speak to that there is plenty of competition about. Your purchase or sale may only be a piddling matter to the solicitor, but the bottom line is that solicitors are operating in a service industry.

The ideal answer is to have a friend who is a solicitor. You can call up after hours and plead 'special relationship'.

Fees

Expect to pay around £400 to £750 plus VAT for purchases or sales of property worth up to £100,000. On transactions involving houses worth more than that the fees are likely to be higher, say, in the £750 to £1,000 bracket. There is no fixed fee scale and solicitors are wide open to competition from other solicitors, not to mention licensed conveyancers, banks and building societies. So it is always possible that you can find an abnormally low quote. Beware, though, that a rock bottom price may mean that your business will get the bare minimum of attention. It will be a mechanical process involving no hand-holding by solicitor and no frills. Do not expect your calls to be answered and expect your file to remain more or less permanently at the bottom of a large pile of papers on the solicitor's desk.

It is advisable, then, to go for a middle ranking quote, or one which will enable you to pick up the telephone at any time and with a clear conscience hassle the person at the other end. Quick reactions from a solicitor can be vital in difficult circumstances, as where a gazumper appears on the scene and your cosy deal degenerates into a 'contract-race' requiring you to exchange immediately in order to secure your purchase. If your solicitor feels he is getting the barest remuneration he may behave with bad grace or, worse, not bother to behave at all, and this may scupper your deal entirely.

DIY CONVEYANCING

The medical equivalent of a routine conveyance would be something as dramatic as paring a corn, and it is difficult to see why people should not indulge in amateur chiropody without going through five years of medical school before they feel qualified to do so. DIY conveyancing may be great fun for those of you for whom the telephone directory is enjoyable reading. But it is a minority activity. The financial arguments for doing it yourself are hardly convincing—on the purchase of a house worth £100,000 you might save yourself the princely sum of £500. You are going to have to read books, ask questions, and generally hustle stupendously slow-moving bureaucrats. If you get off on that sort of thing, you will by the end of the day have the satisfaction of having done something normally reserved to the professional.

The DIY movement's main critic is the Law Society, which represents solicitors. They take a dim view of the inroads being made into what was once the lucrative monopoly of their members and while they have a vested interest therefore in trashing DIY, some of their arguments are difficult to rebut.

They say that if anything goes wrong the DIY enthusiast will have no one but himself to blame. If you find you have parted with a substantial sum only to find that the title of your house is defective, or that the owner of the house next door has the right to drive his car across your garden you might well feel that your solicitor has been negligent. You can always sue. You cannot sue yourself (although maybe your mate/live-in friend could).

The second argument is that if everyone did it themselves, the result would be sheer chaos, and that the system needs the fatherly hand of a solicitor or two to steer a steady course. It is true that do-it-yourselfers depend on there being a solicitor on the other side to do useful things such as acting as a stakeholder for deposit money pending completion.

The DIY mentality is, anyway, light years from that of the Streetwise dealer.

LICENSED CONVEYANCERS

These have only just come into being as an officially approved profession and it is too early to say what we should make of them, or how they will behave, and whether or not their services will be of any reasonable value. One thing that can be said straight off is that they do not possess the expertise in related areas which will be needed if anything goes seriously wrong with your transaction. The solicitor, by contrast, would be able to shift gear from conveyancing mode to a litigation mode. Licensed conveyancers are simply not equipped for all that this would entail and might themselves have to instruct solicitors. In the long run it may not work out as cheaply as you think.

It is indeed difficult to see how conveyancers could offer a significantly cheaper service than solicitors, assuming, as is reasonable, that they have similar overheads in the form of office rent and wages to pay. Of course, a massive put-through of routine conveyances could go far to reducing costs, but solicitors do this anyway. Careful, then, unless your conveyance is routine, and how do you know in advance that it is?

Fees Standard fees of £150-£300 per transaction are talked about, which if matched by reasonable service would be competitive. If not, the economy may be false.

OTHER CONVEYANCERS—BUILDING SOCIETIES AND BANKS

These have just been given the go-ahead to offer conveyancing packages to their borrowers. It remains to be seen how they behave, but they may well rip you off so smoothly you may not even realise it is happening.

The offer will be an entirely 'free' conveyance as part of the service of lending you money, but you can bet that what is given with one hand will be taken away by the other, so watch out for any attempt to recoup the cost by shoving in an additional small percentage on your mortgage rate. By these means they will make even more money out of you than they would if they had charged you a straight fee at the outset. Banks and building societies are, indeed, addicted to scale fees so expect to pay according to the value of the house you are buying. You will also be unable to 'negotiate' a fee with them, unlike a solicitor—the people you will be dealing with simply will not have that kind of mentality. Expect a no frills approach, and bearing in mind their activities in other areas, do not be surprised if they fail to react quickly on your behalf in a difficult situation.

THE ESTATE AGENT—SOLICITOR PARTNERSHIP

There are mutterings that, eventually, restrictions will be lifted on estate agents and solicitors forming partnerships: the 'Little Bang'. Quite who this new breed would act for in a transaction without getting their professional knickers into a complete twist is not easy to surmise. The estate agent's formal relationship is with the seller, but the buyer is where a good deal of the money is in terms of commissions on arranging mortgages, through to life insurance and now, possibly, conveyancing. The last thing the Law Society will permit is for solicitors to represent both buyer and seller in the same transaction—a carpetable offence and an arrangement which would be open to all kinds of abuses, rip-offs and general disservice to the consumer.

THE STREETWISE WAY

The solution seems to be to negotiate the best deal with your solicitor for the straightforward 'no frills' service and leave the essential mechanics of the conveyance to him. But at the same time take a few leaves out of the DIY manual and be ready, if the situation warrants it, to take matters into your own hands.

HOW TO GET THE BEST OUT OF YOUR SOLICITOR

After you have shopped around and agreed the size of the fee, write a letter of instruction saying something to the effect that you would like the solicitor to act for you in the purchase of the house for the fee agreed and that you would like particular attention to be paid to:

● insurance on exchange;

● planning matters not covered by the Law Society's preliminary enquiries form or the search;

● fixtures and fittings;

● rights of way, precise boundaries of the property and ownership of party walls.

None of these are matters which are outside the scope of the solicitor's normal work, and none, therefore, should involve any extra cost. However, by mentioning them at this stage you reduce the likelihood of problems, and if anything does go wrong the solicitor cannot say that there has been no warning.

The draft timetable—the litmus test for the idle lawyer

Send your lawyer a draft timetable along with the letter of instruction. The recipient may smile wryly, file it and never bother to look at it again. You, however, will be working from it and will expect it to be followed. Be reasonable about it so that you cannot be accused of wild optimism. Allow three weeks for the search and preliminary enquiries. At that point you can exchange contracts and completion can take place any time thereafter. If you go for an early completion date there is no reason why the whole process cannot be dealt with in a month, quite reasonable, and with ample time on all sides.

If the solicitor points out that searches are taking six weeks or more to be returned, then be prepared to carry out the search yourself—having checked that this will be acceptable to your source of finance, to your building society or bank.

The whole point of a draft timetable is to enable you to get on the telephone and hassle the solicitor into keeping to it. If the timetable is not followed, you will want to know the reason why.

Remember to agree the dates in advance with your seller, and to supply a timetable so that both solicitors know what is required of them. Any failure to keep to it will be the result either of administrative delay (in which case a personal search could solve matters) or idleness on the part of the lawyers, or both.

Solicitors hate working to timetables, and the more reasonable one is, the fewer excuses they have to deviate from it.

Where things are going too slowly, or going wrong, or you have questions not normally answered by preliminary enquiries or the local authority search, then do not be afraid to pick up the telephone and deal with the matter yourself. The rest of this chapter will cover points that your solicitor should be working on or that you should raise with him or her, and how to ensure you get value for money.

Speeding things up Where you need to move fast and exchange is being held up by a delay in returning the search, call the Local Authority Land Charges Department yourself to hustle them along. There is usually a 'fast lane' for searches—they can be marked 'urgent' if you insist. And you must insist.

The Land Charges people will want to know the date the search was entered, and by whom (give the name of the solicitor's firm—it is a good idea to pretend that you are a solicitor, you get better service). They will give you a best estimate of when the search will be ready.

If they are hopelessly in arrears, then be ready to conduct a personal search (see page 28).

Slowing things down You may actually need to slow down your purchase if your own sale falls through and you have to begin marketing again from scratch. Fortunately, asking a solicitor to move slowly is like inviting a seal to swim—it comes quite naturally. Even at the point of exchanging contracts solicitors can generally do nothing for at least a couple of weeks without causing eyebrows to be raised on the other side. There are always 'further instructions' to be taken and 'enquiries' to be made.

Insurance

Your solicitor must make sure that the house you are buying is insured from the time of exchange of contracts. If the house burns down between the time of exchange and completion the risk is entirely yours and you will still have to come up with the purchase price. If your solicitor negligently fails to see to the insurance, then you could sue him and get his professional indemnity insurance to foot the bill.

Building societies generally insist on insuring a house from the point of exchange in the case of a freehold (they like to cream off the commission); but in the case of a leasehold flat the insurance arrangements will be governed by the lease and it will normally be the landlord's obligation to ensure that the premises are properly insured. Always insist that your solicitor checks.

It is up to the solicitor to let the building society know when contracts are exchanged. (Your solicitor may well be acting on behalf of the building society anyway) but it is worth checking to make sure this is done. In the case of the leasehold, you are covered by some sort of insurance arrangements. You could get yourself named in the policy of the leasehold tenant whose premises you are taking over.

Note that solicitors are under a duty to disclose to you any commission for life insurance or building insurance which they arrange on your behalf. Building societies and banks are not bound by any such rules of behaviour—these are the real fly boys—they will insist on getting the buildings insurance business and stand to make several hundred pounds in any life insurance they arrange on your behalf to cover themselves against the eventuality of your walking in front of a bus leaving the mortgage unpaid. They take you when you come. And they take you when you go.

Problems with preliminary enquiries and the search

Planning permission matters are by general consent not exhaustively dealt with in preliminary enquiries and the search. Preliminary enquiries will tell you whether during the last four years any buildings have been erected on land being sold, or if the house has been added to. The answer from the seller may be a reassuring 'no', but this does not tell you whether proper planning permission existed for any building or addition that went up more than four years previously and which might come to light after you have purchased the house. Unless all structures have been approved you might find, God forbid, that part of the house you've just bought has to be pulled down.

The search does not tell you whether any action or notice is being contemplated by the Planning Department and which they might get round to enforcing once you are the owner.

These points can be checked through by a simple telephone call to the planners. Get your solicitor to do it (write specifically requesting action on this) or do it yourself.

If any action or 'notice' is being contemplated and you still wish to go ahead with the purchase you would be wise at this stage to get a full indemnity from the seller in respect of any failures to obtain necessary permissions for which he was responsible. But everything has its price and the better alternative may be to work out how much it will cost you to comply with the planning requirements, then go back to the seller and negotiate a hefty reduction.

The local search will not tell you whether there are plans afoot for development of adjoining or nearby property.

Again, call the planners and ask them vaguely whether anything is 'going on' in the neighbourhood of the house. They might give you the welcome news that it is about to become a conservation area; they might equally tell you that a supermarket is about to be built on that vacant plot 200 yards away; or there may be nothing to report at all. That extra call is worthwhile.

Fixtures and fittings

Do not expect your solicitor to visit the place you are buying—they should do so but never do, particularly where the conveyance seems routine. Problems can arise over what is being sold with the house or flat.

Fixtures and fittings are a rich source of fruitless arguments. No one seems to know precisely what they are and any nonsense over them will be time and money wasted. It is much better to specify at the very outset whether carpets, light fittings, bookshelves, mixer taps, any attachments at all, are included in the sale. Make a list, copy it, and buyer and seller should give it to their respective solicitors.

Boundary disputes and right of way

If you need to walk over someone else's land to get to another part of your property, say the garage, make sure you have a right to do so. Equally, find out if anyone has a right to walk over your land—developers tend to forget that ancient footpaths are public rights of way.

You might have thought that in an age of high definition satellite photography and computer map-making, we would have been able to tell where one piece of land ends and another begins. But no, of course, ragged edges still abound. Plans relating to unregistered property are only sketch plans; and if the house you are buying is registered land (most residential land now falls into this category) the plan will be to the scale of the Ordnance Survey map (1:1250) i.e. too vague to be of any particular help in resolving a boundary dispute. The Land Certificate (the document of title which goes with Registered Land) actually says that 'the exact line of the boundary will be left undetermined', which of course is no help at all. Solicitors will try to bend the English language in an effort to define what it is that you are buying—'all that parcel of land known as...' goes the phrase—but unless you can measure it out exactly with reference to an obviously identifiable point, the truth is that you will be getting what a consensus of people, of which you are only one, think you are getting. Problems in the country are compounded by disappearing fences, wide ditches, streams drying up and hedgerows getting eaten by cows or obliterated entirely by tractors.

In town, things are better, but not much. It should be easier to tell with the naked eye where the boundary of a property is—a garden wall is, after all, a garden wall. But who owns the wall? Does it belong to you or your neighbour. It may be a party wall, which amounts to shared ownership with the neighbour and therefore shared costs of upkeep. An important question, because whoever owns it has responsibility for its upkeep. In London, a city of walled gardens, machinery for resolving party wall disputes was set up by statute, the London Building Acts 1930-1939. (In other places you have to rely on Common Law.) The plain fact is that when people come to sell a house or garden flat many will have no precise idea of who owns the garden wall, whether it belongs to them, their neighbour, or is shared between them, and answers in preliminary enquiries on these points will often be qualified with the phrase 'to the best of the client's knowledge and belief'.

If in doubt about your responsibilities, visit the people next door and ask them whether they think they own the wall outright or whether it is jointly owned. Very often you will find that both your seller and his next door neighbour are claiming outright ownership of the same wall and if so, you have a problem. If both agree that it is a party wall in joint ownership, then you are okay.

11

AGENTS AND DOUBLE AGENTS

ESTATE AGENTS

Welcome to the new look high street. Gone are the arriviste estate agents with their sharp suits, the flash cars and portable phones. The high street is instead full of boarded-up shops. Agents were among the first casualties of the recession and it is not an uncommon sight to see their former premises on offer through other agents. The good news is that the agents that remain after this environmentally pleasing shake-out are more likely, by the very fact of their continuing commercial existence, to be able to sell property in an active way, as opposed to sitting back and waiting for the offers to roll in. Professionalism will out. And let's be realistic, while you may continue to resent their commission rates, agents are a vital, if occasionally oily cog in the machine.

The newish breed of unqualified estate agent is only distantly related to the old blue-blooded firms of surveyors and land agents which were set up in the nineteenth century to look after large estates of (absentee) landlords, and which gave rise to the profession, properly called, of Chartered Surveyor. However, even firms of Chartered Surveyors are now scuffling away with the best of them (usually at the top end of the market it must be said) selling residential houses and flats for a percentage fee.

Agents are undeniably a source of the commodity you are after. If you are a buyer you put your prejudices (if you have any) to one side and scour all the agents in the area you want to live in as a matter of course. If you locate a house through an agent you then, as buyer, try to seduce the agent into doing the very thing which, as seller, makes them so irritating to deal with. Persuade them to act as double agent. From now on if they want to secure the sale and their percentage fee, they work for you. Usually you find that you are pushing at an open door.

As seller you may first try to sell your house or flat privately, advertising it in precisely the same public places that the agent would do on your behalf—local and (if appropriate) national papers.

Only if this fails will you, as seller, appoint an agent to sell it for you. The crowning irony may be if it has not sold, that it has not sold because it was not sold through an agent. Such is the extent to which quasi-professionalism can mesmerise the public that many people now feel uneasy about striking a private deal precisely because it does not involve an agent. There must be some catch, they think, they must be getting ripped off. If an agent is involved, well, the deal must be okay.

Of course we smile benignly at this kind of naivety and remark that the truth of the situation may be the exact reverse. For good or ill, there is no denying that the Age of Estate Agents has arrived and they seem to flourish, precisely because for ordinary people property transactions are full of unspoken anxieties and the most accurate job description of an estate agent would be hand-holder to both parties involved in the transaction. At worst they can cost a lot of money. At best and if handled properly they can pay for their commission and much more besides.

Even in this largely unregulated world there are standards of behaviour which are unacceptable. Some agents, regrettably, go in for dubious business practices. Beware of the following situations and where possible turn them to your advantage:

- **Unsolicited mailshots** from estate agents telling you that they have 'applicants' wanting 'property' (to include both flats and houses) just like yours. All this tells you, if you did not already know, is that there is good demand in your area. It is a classic technique designed to get a bigger share of the market, and the fact that the agents concerned have the time, inclination and money to spend on mailshots suggests that there may be good reasons why their share of the market is smaller than they would like. Generally these are only sent out by really low-life firms which, in the world of estate agency, is low indeed. File under 'garbage'.

- **Responses to private ads** from estate agents saying they have an applicant for your kind of property. You will have put the ad into a local or national paper with the idea of doing a private deal, and if you genuinely do not want anything to do with agents, put 'no agents' after the telephone or box number, though even this does not prevent the cheekier ones from making the call. Usually the agents are talking clap-trap designed to bring your business their way and have no one in mind at all to bring round to see your property. This is a situation which can work in your favour. Tell them that if they agree to a fee of 1 per cent of the sale price you would be prepared to let them bring their 'applicant' round that afternoon. A number of things can happen: they will try to get a higher percentage out of you by saying that they cannot cover their costs if they agree to less than 2 per cent. You will tell them, depending on how you feel and whether you have had much of a response from private buyers, that it is 1 per cent or nothing or at the very most $1\frac{3}{4}$ per cent. The agent has not yet been born who could turn that deal down—provided of course the 'applicant' genuinely exists. If not, they might politely decline your invitation.

If the agent does bring someone round and an offer is made you can use this in the normal way as a platform from which to build on the price in negotiation with private buyers or with anyone else the agent cares to produce. It is, of course, helpful to be able to say, confidently, 'I already have an offer of X, see if you can improve on it,' and it really does not matter whether the offer comes through an agent or not. All things being equal, you will prefer to do the deal with the private buyer, ultimately, in order to save the agent's fee. Do not feel guilty about using agents in this way. They know full well what the score is and that they can only hope to gain if you have had no interest from private buyers, which is why their first question is always, 'I was wondering if you had any response to your advert in the *Globe* on Sunday?'

• If you do decide to appoint a **sole agent**, always leave the period of the sole agency open. The agent will try to tie you down for as long as possible, three to six months is not uncommon. It is doubtful whether an agent could or would bother to enforce this as a contractual condition but it is an area where needless arguments can be avoided by deliberate vagueness on your part. You want to keep your options as open as possible, which includes sacking the agent or widening the agency to include other agents if and when you so wish. The percentage fee for a sole agency arrangement should be significantly cheaper than the joint agency rate where several agents are competing with each other. If you change from a sole to a joint arrangement expect the agents to put their fees up but do your best to keep them down. Many agents these days want

2 per cent to 3 per cent for joint agency work. When you decide to widen the net tell them they can be agents for 2 per cent or not at all. They have nothing to lose by saying yes, and most will do so if the property seems attractive and easily saleable.

The rate for **joint sole agents** should be exactly the same as for a sole agency, though here you have two agents working for you on a sole agency basis. They will split the fee two thirds to the successful agent and one third to the unsuccessful one, so the arrangement is not all or nothing as far as the agent is concerned. Those arrangements, giving as they do some compensation for the unsuccessful agent, can be criticised as not providing enough incentive for a sale.

• You may be the victim of **territorial warfare** amongst agents. Your house will be advertised with one agent. There will be a knock on the door and an insistent young man or woman will apologise for not having an appointment and will enquire whether it would be possible to show someone round. They are not from the agent you appointed but they noticed the property was for sale. Tell them to go away and make an appointment through your agent. If they are genuine they will do so. If you do show them round it is not uncommon for you to get an offer, although the offer will be conditional of course on your appointing this 'new' agent on their 'usual terms'. They may be satisfied with a joint agency arrangement or may insist on becoming sole agents. The agent will confirm this by letter and soon afterwards the offer will be mysteriously withdrawn. The whole thing was a sham, carefully designed by a pushy agent to muscle in on another's territory, and you will be no further towards your objective of selling your house.

• **Double agents** are not just people who hang around Whitehall or who inhabit the rarefied pages of a Le Carré novel—you can find them on any High Street. Good news for buyers, very bad news for sellers, these are estate agents who regularly reveal the lowest acceptable price a buyer will take to the seller and then put pressure on the seller to accept. The object of course is to secure a quick sale and a painlessly earned commission fee, rather than go to all the trouble of getting the price the seller actually wants, a good few thousand more (a significant sum for the seller but not a large amount in terms of agent's commission).

As a buyer, you want to press the agent as hard as possible into revealing all he knows about the workings of the seller's mind and the lowest acceptable price. As a seller the best way of guarding against this sort of thing is to make quite clear to the agents that their only role in this is to channel potential purchasers through their offices in your direction, and not to negotiate or begin to negotiate. You will handle all that.

• More sinister than the double agents are the **secret agents**. These are the developer or dealer agents who keep the best deals that walk into their High Street offices for themselves or their friends. Usually they look for development properties, and while the seller might think he or she is getting a good price and selling to a genuinely independent third party, in reality he or she will be dealing with a developer with whom the agent has a cosy relationship. This is kick-back territory—the agent will get a fee from the developer and will get to sell the finished units once the development is complete, or he will be selling to the agent himself, at one remove, through the agent's nominee.

Where secret agents are at work ordinary punters will not get a look-in, and the inside deal begins from the very moment the agent steps over the threshold to value the property. The valuation itself will be the price the agent or his developer friends want to pay for it, and it will be carefully pitched so as not to be so ridiculously low that you call in other agents. If the agent offers you extra inducements for a sole agency arrangement—such as a commission rate of 1 per cent or lower—you should be immediately on your guard, the inducement is designed to keep competition at bay. Also, be alert to the demeanour of the agent. They are by nature an optimistic breed and if you find yours wears an expression of long-faced pessimism, shakes his head and begins his summation by saying, 'Well, I don't know Mr/Mrs So and so, I think you'd be lucky to get/you should be very happy with a figure of/you would be wise to accept a sum of £...,' then warning lights should be flashing.

The best way to guard against secret agents is to be wise before the event and get as many agents in at the valuation stage as possible. After valuation you can pick the agent who has quoted you the top price and see how you get on or, indeed, you may decide to go it alone and not use any agents at all. But never, ever put all your eggs in one basket.

That said, the practice of secret agency is not common among the more reputable, longer established firms, and is usually confined to 'cowboy' outfits who mix dealing with selling, although it is worthwhile remembering the saying that 'Behind every great fortune there lies a crime.'

• Even estate agents have to live somewhere and sometimes act innocently on their own behalf in buying a place. This is not the same as 'secret agency' if they level with you and tell you that they are putting in an offer, but there is a clear conflict of interest and they cannot act effectively on your behalf in selling the place. Simply instruct other agents and explain to the agent involved that he or she will have to take their chances along with the rest.

• Agents have a statutory right to ask you, as a buyer who has put an acceptable offer in on a house, to pay a deposit to the agent of up to but no more than £500. This payment is not obligatory nor is it in your interest as buyer to pay it. Simply tell the agent and/ or seller that you are not going to do so, and that your refusal should in no way be interpreted as a lack of interest in going through with the purchase, and that on the contrary you have already started incurring expenses on the purchase by appointing a solicitor and sending off for the local authority search. The agents will not insist on payment or make trouble at this stage. They are much more interested in the pot of gold at the end of the transaction than a sum of money which they will have to repay if the deal goes ahead. As far as you as buyer are concerned you only stand to lose your deposit (if you backed out of the deal for any reason, good or bad), and effectively gain nothing, certainly not the security of knowing that the deal will go ahead. Do not imagine, for example, that if you pay a deposit you will not be gazumped.

• It is usually a complete waste of time having an estate agent's board up outside your property. If buyers are serious they will comb the local agents' ads and discover soon enough that your house is on the market. If you allow a board up the only thing this achieves is free advertising for the agents, who are interested in getting their name known to the general public so that if anyone else in the same street wants to put their house on the market they will know whom to turn to. Of course, agents will tell you that it is vital to have a board up and will talk about the importance of 'passing trade' and 'impulse purchases'. These are rare phenomena indeed and the advantage of having a board outside the house is outweighed by the positive harm it can do to your negotiating position if the board is up for too long (i.e. more than one month) or if, where you have appointed several agents, you allow a forest of boards to be put up. This can be fatal. The question that goes through the buyer's mind as he looks at the boards in your front garden is: 'So many agents and none of them can sell it? Must be something wrong with the place, and/or must be overpriced.'

At the very most, give the 'winning' agent permission to put up a 'sold' sign after contracts have been exchanged.

● You may hear sanctimonious twaddle from the mouths of agents about the immorality of gazumping and contract races, but remember that all agents participate in these practices if they have to and some actually go out of their way to promote them provided that all the 'runners' (applicants) are their own and there is no danger of the business failing into the hands of a competing agent.

● Essentially agents will do what is necessary to secure a sale. If that means running a contract race or promoting a gazump, they will do it. If there are several competing offers around from different agents—precisely the situation which is in the best interest of the seller—then there may be no choice. They might try to avoid gazumping but not, in essence, for reasons of morality but simply because gazumping can get messy and the outcome of the deal may not go their way. They often say that their applicants will not enter into contract races and will withdraw at the merest hint of one. This is usually bullshit designed to bring pressure on the seller to stick with their applicant. For more on gazumping see page 66-68.

● Try to avoid agents whose particulars give a grossly distorted or frankly misleading description of your house. Far better psychologically for a prospective buyer to have a reasonably accurate impression of the house for sale, and to be uplifted by a visit than to arrive and be disappointed.

Equally if you feel the particulars overlook an important aspect of the house's attraction, say so, and get the particulars altered. You can exercise control over the particulars if you insist that the agent sends them to you before they get sent out to the public.

As a buyer you have no comeback against an agent who gives you untruthful or inaccurate details of a house you are buying. Agents' particulars usually contain disclaimers to the effect that no reliance should be placed on them and you will not be able to claim damages for deliberate or negligent misrepresentation if you went ahead on the strength of inaccurate particulars and bought a house. The very most that can be done is to make a complaint to the Trading Standards Office, of which more later.

As a seller, then, make sure the particulars are drawn up to your satisfaction before they are distributed otherwise your house may be more difficult to sell and you will find yourself apologising for the agents' unfortunate grasp of the English language as each prospective buyer walks through your door. If you are a buyer, rely on an inspection and place as little reliance on the particulars as possible. Even beyond the overblown verbiage do not depend on the agent getting such obvious matters as the room sizes correct.

These are often wrong, sometimes deliberately so to give an impression of extra space as in the case of L-shaped rooms where the only width given is the wider rather than the narrower part of the room. Never give any credence to the agent's ideas of age, which can often be embarrassingly wrong. Ignore adjectives like 'period' which can mean anything the agent wants it to mean, even 'period-style', so that a house described as 'period' could just as easily have been built last year as 1750. Where agents' particulars are concerned, the phrase *caveat emptor*, 'buyer beware', really comes into its own.

● If ever you find yourself in the vulnerable position of needing an agent's valuation prior to the purchase of a house, be extra careful that you can approach an agent who can be trusted. This may occur, for example, if you have found a house in an unmortgageable condition which can be done up with a bank loan which, after the works are complete, can be converted into a mortgage. The house will be in essence a development property and the bank manager will need an agent's valuation of what it will eventually be worth before he lends you the money to carry out the works. The agent may charge you a straight fee for a valuation letter of this sort—usually it will not amount to more than £60-£100 on properties worth up to £100,000. Unless he is absolutely trustworthy the danger is that he may go off to his developer friends and the property will be mysteriously snatched from under your nose.

Try to persuade the bank manager that it would be safer to get valuations done *after* you have exchanged contracts. He may see your point of view particularly if the amount he is being asked to lend is more or less secured by the value of the house in its unimproved state. If not, there are two ways to protect yourself against unscrupulous agents.

First choose the most respectable agent you can find to do the valuation—one that would have much to lose by any blemish on his reputation.

Second, see if the seller will give you a short-term option on the property until exchange of contracts. This is a relatively sophisticated manoeuvre which might put some sellers on their guard and suggest to them the possibility that it might be worth more than you are paying. So consider the position carefully and even be honest about your fears if you think it will help.

There is no escaping the fact that obtaining valuations on property not yet bought can be a dangerous game.

● Agents have decided to put their own houses in order: there is now such a thing as an Ombudsman for Corporate Estate Agents whose brief it is to hear complaints about the activities of most large agency groups. He apparently approves of the idea of sellers answering a questionnaire to be passed on by agents to prospective buyers. So, are we about to become more candid about the condition of our houses? Almost certainly not. It will be over the bodies of conveyancing solicitors whose preserve this impinges upon, and the rule, an ultimately streetwise rule, is *caveat emptor*.

RATES OF COMMISSION AND PAYMENT OF FEES

Two per cent would be the upper limit you should pay to a sole agent, and you should try to keep to that limit also if you appoint joint agents.

This may be difficult if the agents get together between themselves and resolve to present a united front—either, they will say, it is 2 per cent or, sorry, mate, we will not do the business.

Much easier is the position where you have agreed a sole agency arrangement at 2 per cent of the deal and the original agent has had a reasonable crack at it but failed to come up with a buyer. You then call the other agents and say, look, if you want an opportunity to sell this house, it is 2 per cent or nothing. They usually go for it. The original agent will be upset, but will understand, if his sole agency becomes a joint agency, and normally does not have the cheek to ask for a raise in percentage commission. If he does, you can tell him that the other agents are on 2 per cent and if he does not want to continue then too bad.

On properties worth around £200,000 or more it is normally possible to agree a fee in advance, which may work out cheaper than the 2 per cent commission. The difficulty here is that if the incentive is entirely removed, service suffers. It is a good idea to talk in terms of 2 per cent up to a certain limit, and 1 per cent thereafter. In theory, then, the agent has a vested interest in obtaining the highest possible price for you.

Agents' commissions can become a bargaining counter with any buyer in a competitive situation. It is sometimes possible to get the winning buyer to pay whatever the eventual price is plus the agent's commission which you, as seller, would have had to pay. Or if not the entire commission, you can agree to 'go halves' on it.

The agent, for you as seller, will send his bill directly to your solicitor once contracts have been exchanged and the agent will expect the bill to be paid on completion. The solicitor should send you a copy of the agent's bill to make sure it is in accordance with your agreement and to make sure you are not being charged too much. Check the bill carefully and make sure VAT has been correctly calculated, then give the solicitor your verdict. If you have any argument with the agent then this is the time to instruct the solicitor not to pay the bill out of the proceeds of sale until the argument is resolved. If the solicitor does pay the agent's fee without consulting you first or contrary to your instructions then he has overstepped the mark and can, if you genuinely did have good grounds for not paying it, be held to account to you for it.

COMPLAINTS

Such statutory controls on the activities of estate agents as do exist have turned out to be unworkable in practice. The Estate Agents Act 1979 set up a system whereby agents can be banned from operating if they have indulged in really gross behaviour and are, in the opinion of the local Trading Standards Office, unfit to be let loose on an unsuspecting public. The Trading Standards Office only acts on complaints from members of the public who are usually unaware that they can complain at all. The result has been that shady agents still operate more or less with impunity. But if you have a complaint you may as well let it be known. You never know your luck. You could also consult a solicitor to see whether you have any legal claim against the agent concerned; and finally, if the agents belong to any professional body (they very well may not) you can take your complaint there too. The leading professional society is the Royal Institute of Chartered Surveyors, whose members are called associates, or, if they are more senior, fellows. They are entitled to have the letters ARICS or FRICS after their names. Chartered Surveyors have passed a series of stringent professional tests and are theoretically capable of doing much more than just sell houses. Though there are bad apples in every barrel, this particular one probably contains fewer than most.

Equally anxious to maintain standards is the National Association of Estate Agents. Again its members are either associates or fellows, so you may see ANAEA or FNAEA after their names.

It is debatable whether a rogue agent would have his nose, or his business, put seriously out of joint by strong words of censure or even ejection from any national association, but you can try it.

12

SURVEYORS

It is the surveyor's job to find out whether the bow in that wall means a collapse is imminent after all these decades, and so on, and generally to give you enough information about a house so that you can form a decision as to whether or not to buy.

Reduce the possibility of foul-ups by using a chartered surveyor or a qualified architect. In negotiations with the seller the more letters your adviser has after his name the better, and certainly, if the bank requires a structural survey, they will expect it to be given by someone properly qualified to do so. Either discipline—architecture or surveying proper—will cover the ground.

There is one type of surveyor but there are two types of surveys: the Valuation Survey and the Full Structural Survey. The valuation survey tells you whether if you need a mortgage you can buy the house, and the structural survey tells you whether you ought to or not. Both can be useful to you in negotiating a lower price with the seller.

VALUATION SURVEYS

The purpose of a valuation survey is to enable the lenders (whether bank or building society) to check to their satisfaction that the proposed loan is less than the value of the property in its present condition, so that if the worst happened and they foreclose, the amount of the loan would be fully covered by the sale price.

Valuers are paid to be cautious. These are people who will ensure that any recovery in the housing market is slow and tentative. Fully 25 per cent of deals in the South East fell apart during the Recession because of low valuations. This situation is not helped by the fact that valuers often have little or no local knowledge and depend on local agents for guidance on property values. So serious has this problem become that a group of concerned surveyors have formed themselves into the Independent Surveyors' Association, with the express aim of countering down-valuing by uninformed, non-local valuers. See Useful Addresses for details.

When he walks through the door of the house you want to buy, the valuation surveyor knows exactly how much you intend to borrow off the lender and what the agreed sale price of the property is. However, the valuation surveyor is not working directly for you, and although you are paying for his services you do not have a right to read his report.

You may also find that the surveyor suggests a 'retention' on part of the mortgage loan to be advanced to you until remedial building works have been completed. Or the house may simply 'fail' the survey—in terms of either its price and its condition— and be plain unmortgageable.

Whatever the outcome, the valuation survey is useful to you in the following respects:

● On the price you are paying, it is a useful, though usually very conservative, second opinion.

● The survey may indicate that work needs to be done on the house and more costs incurred in doing so. The lender may even make a retention of part of the loan before the full amount of the work is done. In the first case the work to the house is optional but desirable, in the second it is vitally necessary before you get your full loan, but in both cases this result enables you to go back to the seller to negotiate a reduction in price.

● Provided the property is not inherently unmortgageable but only unmortgageable for the amount of loan you need, you can turn even a 'failed' valuation survey to your advantage by renegotiating with the seller.

Retentions and reinspections

The valuation surveyor may recommend that a certain amount of the mortgage loan be retained pending remedial work to the property. This is not an outright refusal but, effectively, the property is going to cost you more than you thought unless, of course, you realised from the outset that work needed to be done and had worked this into the calculations of what your offer price should be.

A 'retention' is generally the signal for you to go along to your bank (which may also be lending you the mortgage) to take out a straight commercial loan for the work, the loan to be repaid once the work is completed to the satisfaction of the lender, who will send round a valuation surveyor for a 'reinspection' of the property when you give them the word that it has been done. If all is well, then the lender releases the balance of your mortgage and you repay the bank the loan you took out.

The lender usually insists that the work is carried out, but sometimes they do not, in which case you can choose whether or not to do it. You may decide not to if the work does not affect the marketability of the house and is otherwise not fundamental to your well-being.

Occasionally the lender may extend the full amount of the mortgage you need on the basis that you attend to certain minor matters within a stated period following completion. You may be given six months, for example, to replace cracked slates on the roof, or to redo defective electrical wiring, or to repaint the exterior. In these circumstances, provided you keep up with your repayments, the lender will often 'forget' to reinspect and do not be surprised not to hear from them. They are busy falling over themselves to lend money to people and the question of the electrical circuitry in your downstairs lavatory is not at the top of their agenda.

'Failed' surveys

If the lender turns down your mortgage application after the valuation survey then the message is that the resale value of the house does not cover the amount you intended to borrow. You should find out why not, and most building societies or bank managers will tell you, and some will even send you a copy of the report (though they do not have to).

It may turn out that the valuer thought the property was over-priced. If so go back to the seller, and negotiate. If the seller is under pressure to sell you are in a strong position to bring the price down. If it comes down far enough you can go back to the lender and, relying on the valuation survey already carried out, see whether the figures now alter in your favour.

Or it may be that the surveyor has discovered something sinister about the property. And if on hearing this news you still want the house, you can sometimes salvage a deal from an apparently hopeless situation. Go back to the seller and try to negotiate a substantial reduction in the price of the house, taking into account the full cost of the works to be done. If the seller is desperate enough, and if you are successful, you can go back to your lenders and tell them that your mortgage requirement will initially be one figure with a further sum to be retained by the lender pending completion of, say, the underpinning work which you will undertake yourself as soon as you have bought the house.

There is, of course, a lot of hassle involved here. However, in order to protect their building society clients, valuation surveyors' estimations of how much remedial work there is to be done are notoriously pessimistic and their calculations of the costs involved are also usually high. The opportunity here, then, is to negotiate the price reduction with the seller on the basis of the mortgage valuer's high figures, and then to get the job done cheaper.

The valuation price

The valuation price is usually less than the sale price unless the seller has got his valuation wrong and you are getting a particularly good deal. Lenders know this and indeed expect their valuation surveyors to err on the side of caution in making valuations. If the surveyor gets it wrong and overvalues a house which is later repossessed and sold by the lender for less than the amount loaned, the surveyor can expect to have to pay the difference out of a claim on his professional indemnity insurance. There is general caution all round and valuation prices are generally shy of the market price. Rarely does the valuation price exceed the sale price, in which case you, as buyer, are getting a very, very good deal.

As seller, you should do your best to find out whether the valuation price came anywhere near the asking price. Ask the agents, who will after all be working for you, and the buyers *precisely* what the figure was. If it approximated the valuation price or exceeded it, then you should consider very carefully whether or not you have underpriced your property. Buyers are usually so relieved that the valuation has gone okay that they will tell you or find out from their building society for you what the exact valuation price was.

Speed

The surveyor will call up the seller to arrange a time to view. Once it has been done the surveyor writes his report and forwards it to the lender (bank or building society) who then processes the report, studies the recommendations and generally takes time before making you a formal mortgage offer. It is reasonable to expect an off-the-cuff 'verbal' assessment of how the valuation went within a day or two, or if you insist, the same day. It is simply a question of the building society or bank manager making a call to the surveyor who knows what is expected of him and can give the 'okay' or not, then and there over the telephone. Insist.

The survey itself

This is High Noon for the seller as well as the buyer. As seller you will have made discreet visits to your local DIY shop and will have taken all steps necessary to divert attention from the bowing flank wall (you hope the surveyor takes the view that it is 'historic' and no longer moving) and the sinister cracks that have developed on the wallpaper as a result; and you will have jammed the sash windows shut so that they do not vibrate with every passing car.

The surveyor may walk round the property and be out again and this may take less than ten minutes. He knows what to look for and will generally not be taken in by idle conversation or offers of tea. Do not be surprised if, in older houses, he jumps up and down in every room. He is testing for movement in the joists and evidence that they are no longer firmly embedded in the walls, the usual symptoms being springy floorboards and rattling windows.

Surveyors are, however, human and are more likely to value the place highly if they like the 'feel' of it. It is worth tidying a place up, but stop short of expensive redecorations unless of course you are hiding damp patches and papering over cracks.

It is also worth asking the surveyor straight out what he thinks of the place. 'I don't like it,' is a common response and you should brace yourself for what are, quite literally, home truths. A trenchant criticism of the place you live in does not necessarily mean that the house has failed its valuation. Surveyors are a habitually envious lot and no professional knows better than they how well some people have done through the recent surge in prices. If they are going to fail the place it is unlikely that they will tell you there and then—it is a breach of his duty of confidentiality to his client (the lender); but if the valuation is clearly acceptable, he may say something vague like 'I shouldn't think you'll have any trouble with this,' or 'It should be okay.' They know you are nervous about the outcome, so do not be afraid to ask.

Costs

Building societies and banks have a set scale of fees and you should expect to pay around £300 for a valuation survey. If you are fortunate enough to be allowed to appoint your own valuation surveyor then it should work out cheaper. Surveyors' usual rates are somewhat lower than the figure the bank or building society like to charge. But check beforehand to make sure the 'usual' rates are not more expensive.

STRUCTURAL SURVEYS

The day after you buy your house you put a foot through a floorboard and discover that the place is riddled with dry rot. Ah! You think to yourself, ever optimistic, not to worry, that was not mentioned in the survey—I'll sue the surveyor. But you read the report and discover that the surveyor only undertook to report on any *visible* defects, and the dry rot was *not* visible, it was lurking in a recess under a floorboard. Too bad, says the surveyor, any defects lurking in covered recesses are entirely at the client's risk! But you say, you cannot have paid £450 to be told nothing you did not already know about the property. Tough luck. You did.

Structural surveys are a great idea in principle but usually turn out to deliver much less than they should. They are designed to give an accurate picture of the state of a property so that you can make up your mind whether or not to go ahead and buy it. Also, they are supposed to provide some sort of insurance against defects which emerge after you move in. As we have seen, unless the defect which the surveyor has missed is so gross that you could practically fall over it, the chances are that they will avoid liability. The truth is that surveyors only report on problems which are perfectly obvious to the informed layman.

The structural survey itself is a detailed report which can run to 20 pages or more and will be full of strange architectural and building terms which will mean nothing to you unless you speak the language. Either right at the beginning or right at the end the surveyor will list his get-out clauses which effectively exempt him from liability for any defects not immediately visible. So, though he may poke about in the basement or the attic *if* he can get access (it may not be available), do not expect him to take up so much as a carpet let alone a floorboard to see what lies beneath. Much of the report will set out information which you already know— you will be told how many rooms there are and the sizes will be carefully noted in metres and feet—or which is of general interest, such as whether the foundations arc alluvial shingle or clay deposits (interesting, perhaps, but not vital to your interests unless as a result the house is likely to cave in).

What the survey does not do is give you a definitive answer to the vital question, 'Should I buy this property?' To be fair, it is not an issue on which the surveyor is best qualified to make a definitive recommendation, because buyers can handle problems in different ways, some being more robust than others. Rebuilding a flank wall might mean a 'no buy' for some clients, while others will simply take it in their stride. Who is to say what the client should do? Surveyors see their task as presenting the full picture of the property and leaving the final decision to the client.

What the surveyor can and should do is to make an itemised and *priced* list of the work which, in his estimation, needs doing. This will enable you to work out what you will have spent on the property, including the purchase price, once all necessary work is done. If this adds up to more than the house would fetch on the open market, then in commercial terms, the deal is a non-starter.

This is the point at which the survey can be of practical use. Armed with a list of work to be done, you can go back to the seller and negotiate a lower sale price. If the seller argues that the cost of work needing to be done has already been discounted in the (relatively) low asking price, you should ask yourself, if it is true, whether you really need bother to go to all the trouble of buying a place which needs money spending on it when you could buy a place in good condition straight away for the same price. Mention this to the seller. When he sees the sale slipping from his grasp he may come back and offer you a discount.

Remember that the surveyor's estimate of what needs to be done is always pessimistic and priced on the expensive side. This is a factor which works in your favour. Your negotiations to reduce the sale price will be on the basis that you will have to spend the amount set out in the report, but in fact you may be able to get away with paying much less, and indeed, unless the work to be done is of vital structural significance, you may decide not to bother doing it all which is, after all, your prerogative.

If the work is structural then in all likelihood it will be carried out under the supervision of the local authority's District Surveyor (the DS) who will decide the precise extent and nature of any remedial work, and you will have no choice but to sing to the DS's tune.

If you know in advance that you are going to use the survey for price reduction you can specifically request the surveyor to be even more pessimistic on the costs than he might ordinarily be. He will be only too happy to oblige. This gives you even more room for manoeuvre, compromise and generous deal-clinching gestures such as an offer to 'split the difference' with the seller and reduce the price by half the amount of the surveyor's estimate of the cost of the works.

If some of the works suggested by the report are minor, or decorative, you can offer the seller the option of seeing to them himself before completion if he thinks he can save money. If the seller does agree to undertake work to the house before completion you should, as buyer, try to ensure that he does by getting it included as a condition in the Contract of Sale, so that completion will only take place once the outstanding works have been completed. Expect stiff resistance from the seller's solicitor who will want as few conditions in the contract as possible.

Getting the best out of your surveyor

Specifically instruct the surveyor not to bother giving you a long recital of what the house consists of—you can see that perfectly well for yourself even though you may not possess the precise architectural/building terminology to describe it. That should save some money. Rather get the surveyor to concentrate on defects, structural or cosmetic, and to give you a breakdown of the cost of putting each defect right. The survey you want will be designed to give you ammunition for negotiations with the seller, it will be a great deal shorter and, you will argue, should be less expensive. Try for a price of not more than £200, or even less if you can get it. Remember that in so far as he misses any defects he should have seen, the surveyor will still remain liable to compensate you, so do not expect him to give his services away.

You will be obliged by a bank to have a structural survey done on the house you are buying (and conceivably also on the house you are selling) if you are borrowing an open-ended bridging loan to enable you to complete the purchase of the house you are buying before your own house has been sold. The bank will want to be entirely satisfied that the amount of its loan could be recouped by the sale of either property if anything goes seriously wrong, as it may very easily do if you find that your own sale does not go ahead as planned. (For more details see the Bridging chapter on page 88.)

Claims against the surveyor

Very occasionally a surveyor misses a defect which, even on his own narrow definition of his responsibilities, he should have seen. An example might be the failure to diagnose a bowed exterior wall as still moving, or the failure to detect fungal infections and rot in an accessible part of the house such as the roof space or the basement.

If this happens the surveyor is liable to compensate you for the full amount of the cost of putting the defect right, and he will in turn probably make a claim against his professional indemnity insurance. The claim against the surveyor would be in addition to any other claims you may have under your building's insurance; or under an NHBC guarantee (if the property is a recently converted flat on a newly built house and is covered by National House Builders insurance protection); or, if appropriate, under any guarantees for woodworm, damp or dry rot which may exist; or under any legislative provision, such as the Defective Premises Act 1972, which gives you rights to claim damages for defects in a property caused by the negligence of the builder who built or converted it. In the last two instances you will have problems if the builders are no longer trading or have gone bankrupt.

Specialist surveyors

Specialist surveyors can be brought in to advise on the severity of any particular problem once it has been documented in the report and if the surveyor advises it. You might, for instance, approach a **quantity surveyor** to give a more precise estimate of the cost of works, or a **structural engineer** for advice on the feasibility of major rebuilding works; and specialist firms of **pest eradicators** can be called upon to give reports on the extent and elimination of insect infestation, dry or wet rot, and damp control.

The reports of the quantity surveyor and the structural engineer will cost you at least as much as the structural survey, but the pest and damp control estimate is free. Again, as in the case of the structural survey, it should be possible to recover any fees paid if as a result of these reports you are able to talk down the purchase price of the house.

13

ARCHITECTS

Vanity, vanity, all is vanity. But architects are deserving of human kindness and sympathy (if not employment). Of all the professions afflicted by the recession, theirs has been the worst hit. In 1992, around 40 per cent of trained architects were unemployed or semi-employed. Look hard at your acupuncturist—he may be an architect on the side. With notable exceptions architects tend to be a narcissistic and inward-looking lot, and are, as a result, much misunderstood and maligned. They have also been arguing with clients, usually over money, for longer than anyone might care to think about. One of the most famous rows involved Vanbrugh and the Duchess of Marlborough. After Blenheim Palace was finished in 1725, after 20 years of building, she refused to let him near the place.

On the whole architects have failed to impress on the public the integrity of their motives and there is a yawning gap between their image of themselves and the public's perception of them. Ironic, because theirs is the profession most sensitive to criticism, and the one most in need of popular approval.

The problem seems to be that architects work in the area of taste (which lawyers and doctors do not, with the possible exception of the plastic surgeon), and taste is something we all like to think we possess. This is the first arena for potentially explosive differences. Guard against this by making it very clear from the outset precisely what you want the architect to do, and precisely how much latitude there will be for the architect's self expression. Talk about every aspect of the job well in advance and impose as much of your own taste as you feel like doing or (important) that the planners will let you get away with. At the end of the day the architect will be in the position of taking your instructions, and translating your wishes first into plans, then into bricks and mortar, and any question of the architect having done 'this' when you would have preferred 'that' will simply not arise. Good clients are firm and say what they want, and the firmer you can be with your architect, the better the service you will get (which will include advice if your instructions are obviously silly).

So why have one?

Before you buy a place, an architect can give you a roughly accurate idea of the complexity of any work that needs to be done, and you can then decide whether or not to go ahead with the purchase.

Once in occupation, or sometimes after purchase but before physically moving in, you may decide to carry out work on a property which involves obtaining planning permission, or getting builders' quotes.

Phase I of the architect's job is to draw up plans and on the strength of these apply to the local authority's planning department for planning permission.

Phase II relates to the building works and may involve further drawings, known as **working drawings**, which are for the benefit of the District Surveyor, the Structural Engineer, and the builders themselves. At this stage the architect makes a **specification** which is a detailed list of the works. On the basis of the specification and the working drawings the architect can take in quotes from a number of builders. Between you, you decide on the best quote, and go ahead.

Phase III of the architect's brief will be to supervise the project once the builders are 'on site', to make sure the district surveyor is happy about the progress of works and that they are in conformity with the building regulations. He will check that the proper materials are being used and that work is generally done in what is called 'a good and workmanlike' manner.

You can hire an architect for any or all of these phases. It may be that you think you can 'project-manage' the work yourself, and that you only need the architect to draw up plans and guide the planning application through to a successful conclusion. If you really think you can cope with the builders yourself (see pages 142-152) then of course you will save money in architect's fees.

CHOOSING AN ARCHITECT

In any event make sure the architect you use belongs to RIBA (The Royal Institute of British Architects) or their rival organisation the Association of Chartered Architects. These are the main professional organisations, and membership of them attests to basic competence in the area. If the job is grand enough (it may be difficult to feel inspired about a lounge extension) consult an architect or two and see whether you like their previous work. There are horses for courses, and it is no good appointing an architect who specialises in inner city refurbishment and conversion work if you are proposing to build a small country house in the Cotswolds. Most architects have local knowledge and—this can be vital—connections with planning departments. Always ask whether they get on well with the planners, and the response you most want to hear is: 'We have never yet had a planning application turned down,' although that could be because they have only been operating for three months. Check.

Fees

When they have it their own way, architects' fees will be linked by percentage to the cost of the project, which is likely to vary upwards rather than down. For this very good reason you should resist this percentage link and impose as early as you can in your relationship a lump-sum fixed fee for the job.

The architects will be lusting after a fee of around 10 per cent of the total cost of the project, particularly if they are asked to perform work in all three phases of the project (see page 136).

They may attempt to hustle you by citing the RIBA's scale of recommended fees. The answer to this is simply that there is too much competition about from non-chartered architects and draftsmen and too many proper architects chasing what work there is in the private sector for the RIBA to impose its fee-scale on the public, and the word is, as with solicitor's fees for conveyancing—negotiate.

For work in Phase I try to limit the cost to 3 per cent. This would mean, for instance, that for making plans and obtaining planning permission for a job costing £35,000 the architect would make £1050. A reasonable sum in view of the likelihood that the plans involved for works costing this amount are not likely to be particularly difficult or time-consuming, certainly nothing that a competent architect could not knock out in a couple of days. The planning matters will take longer, and there may be amendments to be made to the drawings as a result of the architect's consultations with the planning officers. But at that price, why not?

For Phase I and II work, 5 per cent of the total cost of the project is reasonable. On the example of work costing £35,000, the architect's fee would amount to an extra £1750, plus VAT of course, and so far the builder would not have set foot inside the house.

For work through all three phases, never pay more than 7 per cent of the total cost of the project and less if you can negotiate it. On building costs of £35,000, 7 per cent works out at £2450 which is an entirely reasonable sum which only an extremely spoilt architect (i.e. one that works on local or central government contracts) would turn down.

Fixing the fee

Abide by the golden rule and get more than one architect to estimate costs—three is a workable number. At your first meeting with each architect put your cards on the table and tell them that you are taking estimates of the cost of the works from other architects. Get each of them to give you a ball park estimate of what the works will cost and having worked out whatever 3, 5 or 7 per cent of the total cost is, and how much of the project you want the architect to participate in, tell them straight how much you are prepared to pay. You do not refer to percentages or encourage the architect to do so, and the best way of negotiating here is not to negotiate. If the architect starts mumbling about 10 per cent you very politely say that if the job cannot be done for the sum you mentioned then reluctantly you will have to go elsewhere. You also point out that unless the building costs turn out to be dramatically in excess of the figure the architect has estimated you would not expect to pay any extra for the architectural work. For instance, if the architect estimates the cost of the works at £35,000, then your fee to him for the whole job would remain the same, unless quotes came in at say, £45,000. You may find agreement on this more difficult but try it all the same. Of course, if the builders' quotes are way in excess of the architect's original, back-of-fag-packet estimate of costs then you may wonder about the architect's competence. Also, it is not difficult to see that architects would have an interest in swinging their own deals with builders in return for recommending a quote to a client.

Sometimes an enticingly low original estimate of cost of works can be explained by an architect's desire not to disappoint or frighten away a potential client with high figures. They are counting on the fact that once committed you will have no choice but to see the project through to completion and along the way you can be gradually eased into the realisation that the cost of works is more expensive than you had imagined. Your first line of defence against this is the fact that you will be seeking the views of other architects and it is likely that you will get a realistic picture, or something approaching it, out of at least one of them. The second line of defence is simply to re-examine the whole business before you accept any high quotes from builders which your 'low-estimate' architect has recommended.

Confirm any fee arrangement by letter once it has been agreed. Do not leave this to the architect who may 'forget' the details of your arrangement and charge at the higher RIBA rate. Specify in your letter precisely what the architect will be expected to do for his fixed fee (i.e. one that will not vary upwards if the project turns out to go over budget). At all costs *avoid* paying the architect on an hourly basis—it is almost always the cause of friction, and one or other party ends up feeling ripped off. Rates of £25-£30 per hour are usually quoted and it is, of course, difficult to expect complete accuracy or authenticity in keeping a track of the precise hours worked.

Staged payments

Budget on payment of a proportion of the architect's total agreed fee at the end of each phase. The first payment, therefore, would be on submission of plans for planning permission (provided the architect gives an undertaking that the plans will be redesigned and resubmitted if they are not acceptable or in some way not up to standard); the second payment would be made when the architect has drawn up 'contractual documents' (the specification and working drawings) and completed negotiations with a suitable builder. Note here that working drawings, particularly in small jobs where the cost of works is under £100,000, can sometimes be dispensed with. At the less sophisticated end of the builders' spectrum, and particularly in conversion work, there is not a great deal of precise reading of plans and the plans used for planning permission are usually sufficient to give the builder the idea of what is required of him.

When you make the final payment do not do so immediately the works have come to an end. Wait for the certificate from the District Surveyor and the Environmental Health Inspector (if and where appropriate) to arrive before writing your final cheque out to the architect.

THE ARCHITECT AS 'BUFFER'

If you decide to make use of the architect's Phase III services, he will become your special agent in dealing with the builder whose quote you have accepted. You will rely on the architect to produce **certificates** valuing the builder's work from time to time, and it is these certificates which will indicate how much you should pay to the builder. By employing an architect you are able to say with conviction to the builder, 'Don't argue with me, argue with the architect.'

Expect the architect to hold **site meetings** regularly with the builder. You could turn up to these and participate if you so wished. You should insist that minutes of the site meetings be kept as a record of who was there, what matters were discussed and what was decided upon. If you cannot be at the site meetings, insist that you be sent copies of the minutes.

INSURANCE

Make sure the architect has full **professional indemnity insurance**. Because it is so expensive (up to £3000 per year for one architect) some do not go in for it. Should anything go seriously wrong with the works and if there is any question of negligent supervision or a fault in design, you want to be able to put the architect in the firing line along with the builder, and be reasonably sure of getting some compensation. If the architect is uninsured you may get nothing even though you could win your case.

ARCHITECT'S CONTINUING LIABILITY

If anything goes wrong with the building work once the job has finished it is comforting to know that in the right circumstances you may be able to sue either or both the architect and the builder.

Architects have continuing liability for building work which they have designed and for which they are responsible to supervise. The waking nightmare of most architects is that one of the buildings they have designed will fall down or otherwise turn out to develop some appalling defect which they should have anticipated and prevented. The worst does happen sometimes—Ronan Point of infamous memory.

Continuing liability is bad news for architects but reasonably comforting news for you, though their liability may be limited to some extent if you have accepted the architect's standard form for Conditions of Engagement. This is published and revised periodically by the RIBA and provides that although there may be a requirement to make regular site visits, the architect cannot be held responsible for the builder's failure to perform his contract; and while the architect should make sure that the work is done as well as possible, exhaustive inspections of the builder's work are not his responsibility. These conditions are intended to limit the architect's liability for negligent supervision and they should not be accepted without question or modification, or, if you like, at all.

You may be in a slightly different position where you have bought a house or a flat from someone (a private individual or maybe a developer) who recently employed an architect or builder to carry out works. Under the Defective Premises Act 1972, if some serious defect in the works appeared you may be able to sue the architect and builder even though no strict contractual relationship existed between you. There may be enormous problems of proof and enormous practical problems if the architects are no longer practising (or if the builder is no longer trading or has gone bankrupt) and you should check with a solicitor to see whether the remedies available in theory are worth following up.

14

Builders

'To build is to be robbed' said Dr Johnson. A little extreme maybe. But if any occupation deserved a government health warning, this is it. Builders suffer from a number of occupational weaknesses which can be damaging to your health, mental and physical, and are certainly hazardous to your bank balance. Approach them with care; and, if you can, try to wear the conversational equivalent of a condom. Hear what is said but do not let it touch you. Respond in the normal way but beware that anything you are told by a builder may be meaningless in the conventional sense.

There is no substitute for battle experience. So take a deep breath and remember this—you cannot tell how deep a puddle is until you step into it.

CHOOSING A BUILDER

In the post-recessionary world most builders are available for work. There is, obviously, a streetwise advantage to be had in terms of shopping round for the hungriest, lowest (which does not necessarily mean the best) quote. Those that come to you by personal recommendation should be best but often turn out to be disappointing and if things go badly wrong you can ruin a friendship. You may, of course, be recommended a builder by your architect if you use one but remember that this is kick-back territory and there is no harm in getting alternative quotes. Consult your local authority works department—they know of reputable local builders; or close your eyes and stab a needle into the Yellow Pages (if you choose one this way do not be afraid to ask for references); or consult a trade association and ask them to recommend a member.

There are a number of trade associations covering the building industry but often anybody prepared to pay the subscription fee can be a member, and membership itself provides no certainty of quality workmanship. However, the leading associations—the Building Employers Federation and the Federation of Master Builders—do operate schemes which benefit and protect the unsuspecting punter.

All members of the BEF are required to offer customers the possibility of participating in the guarantee scheme, which covers work valued between £500 and £30,000. If the original BEF member fails to complete the job for any reason or does it badly, the work will be completed by another BEF member, and any additional costs caused by defective workmanship are covered up to a cost of £5000. The price of the scheme is 1 per cent (minimum £20) of the job price and you should make sure that the particular type of work you want done is covered (not all are).

The Federation of Master Builders operates a similar scheme under similar terms, but not all members of the FMB participate in it—in fact only a minority (about 1500) of their total membership of around 20,000—so check that your FMB member is a participator before taking a quote. If he is you will be reassured to know that he will have been in business at least three years and will have been vetted by the FMB for business methods and quality of workmanship.

Quotations and estimates

It goes without saying that you should always try to tie a builder down to a price before work starts, and that you should never let work begin without having some idea of the price. What you want out of a builder is a 'quotation' rather than an 'estimate'.

There is a fundamental difference between the two which you must be aware of in any dealings with a builder.

A quote is essentially an undertaking to do a job at the quoted, fixed price, while an estimate is only a vague figure of what the builder thinks he can do the job for. In theory estimates can vary either way but in practice it varies only one way—upwards. Builders, particularly of the cowboy variety at the lower end of the scale, are often themselves unaware of the difference between quotes and estimates. For them the problem has usually never arisen, for they have never kept to a fixed price in their working lives. Ordinary members of the public are usually not aware of the difference between a quote and an estimate and the cowboy builder would be stunned if somebody actually suggested he keep to a price.

Estimates leave you wide open to rip-offs, and you should always ask for a quote. It has to be said that in practice when you are dealing with a hand-to-mouth subcontractor whose only asset is his work in progress (i.e. your job) then the difference between quotes and estimates becomes academic. For all practical purposes you can forget the legal niceties and the best way of ensuring that the work is done is to keep a very firm grip on payments and to make sure that you only part with money when work is properly completed.

Specification

The quote should always be tied into a detailed specification and plans which should be decided on before any work starts.

You will hear builders and architects talk about the 'spec' (pronounced 'spess') which is the slang term for the specification and it is usually to be read in conjunction with architects' plans and comprises a full list of the work to be done, with materials to be used, together crucially with prices for each phase of the operation. Some builders are quite capable of drawing up their own spec if you give them plans but if you leave them to their own devices and if they know that the spec is not going to be subject to the scrutiny of any other professional, then you can expect high prices.

Even if you are operating without an architect, you should insist that any quote for a builder is broken down into its constituent parts. When all your quotes are in (three or four is a workable number), compare them and see where each quote has an advantage over another. Then go back to the builder and ask how he worked out each part of the quote, on the basis of man hours, time spent, rates of pay and so on. In this way it is sometimes possible to whittle the price down but remember that you will be starting from scratch in a complicated subject and you will be at a severe disadvantage. Your interests therefore may be better served by appointing an architect (or a quantity surveyor) to negotiate with the builder on his quote. A good architect can more than pay for his fee in this way.

Finishing dates and damages for late completion

You must anyway get the builders to agree to finish by a particular date. It focuses their minds on the schedule and keeps them at it. Unfortunately the law says that unless you state categorically that 'time is of the essence' in your agreement (which is legal jargon for saying that the date for finishing the works is a term of the contract), the agreed finishing date will be no more than a date by which both parties hope that the work will be finished, which is essentially no help to you at all.

But if it is stated that 'time is of the essence' then unless the builders finish by the agreed date they may be liable to pay you 'liquidated' damages, which are damages which can be measured in precise financial terms rather than damages which, although they may be very real, are much more difficult to quantify (such as damages for general inconvenience). A good example of liquidated damages would be the extra costs incurred in renting another house (or hotel bills) until your own house is ready to move into.

MAKING A CONTRACT

Theoretically you can make a contract for building work, as with any contract not involving land, by word of mouth, though if you did so the result could be disastrous. In these circumstances the builder has more or less a *carte blanche* to name his price, and to finish when he likes. If things go wrong you can, of course, protest that your agreement was quite different, but you will have problems of evidence and it may well come down to 'your word against his'. Your only remedy in these circumstances is to withhold payment.

The best advice is to get the builder to submit a written quotation, and then to respond by letter confirming the arrangements, including the price, the finishing date and the fact that time is of the essence. Do what some people forget to do, keep a copy of the letter.

Progress payments

Always pay the builder in arrears. Even with the help of a detailed specification it will be difficult for you alone to assess how much work has been done or to decide whether or not it has been done. You can assume that the builder will always ask for more than he deserves and in this situation you run the grave risk of falling out. You should never be in a situation of having paid for more work than has actually been done but, if you are, make sure you have someone other than yourself and the builder to blame. An architect will do nicely. The architect should check each item off against the specification as and when it is completed properly, issue a certificate enabling you to make the progress payments, and he should provide for retentions of any money for work not properly carried out.

Defects period

Either because you are extremely sensible, or on the advice of your architect, you will, by the end of the job, still owe the builder between 10 and 20 per cent of the cost of the works. This you will release to him once the defects period has expired and provided nothing has come to light in that time which suggests that the job was done negligently. If a defect does appear then you can get the work done and deduct the cost from the final payment to the builder. The defects period usually lasts three months, but pitch for six months and see if you can get the builder to agree.

Insurance

Loosely fitted slates have a habit of falling on the heads of unsuspecting passers-by and visitors tend to stick their feet through ceilings or step into black voids where once there was a floor. Builders are by no means above damaging neighbours' property: holes frequently appear through to the house next door. You will be at the top of the list of people to be sued. You will, of course, say that the builder was responsible and will pass the buck, but unless the builder is properly insured you might find yourself paying damages to the injured party. Expensive.

As far as you are concerned, disaster can be avoided by proper insurance. Before work begins you will want to see evidence that the builder is insured against any personal injury claims or claims for damage to property. Do not be satisfied with a bland verbal assurance. It is vital, and quite normal, to ask for a photocopy of the builder's certificate of insurance.

Extras and omissions

It may well be that you authorise work to be done which is not included in the specification. Provided the extras are properly authorised you will be bound to pay, but unless you do properly authorise them you are not technically under an obligation to pay the builder for extra work which he has undertaken on his own initiative and without reference to you.

Always make sure that 'extras' are what they claim to be and are not in fact what the builder was already bound to do, dressed up in a different guise. The argument about what is and what is not an extra can normally be settled if the spec is clear and complete. Make it clear to the builder that you will only pay for an extra if he consults you in advance and you authorise it. It should, for example, be clear whether foundation work needs to be done and any structural problems should have been thought about well in advance. Dry rot may be more difficult to detect, and sudden, unpleasant discoveries are sometimes made which involve extra costs. Ideally any extras you incur should be entirely optional, involving matters of taste rather than necessity.

Against extras you may be able to set off a larger number of omissions, with the result that the overall cost might actually turn out to be less than the figure you originally anticipated. It does happen. Much depends here on how cleverly the specification has been drawn up and how effectively the subsequent building work is supervised. Much better to take a pessimistic view at the outset and be able to clock up omissions rather than take an optimistic view and fall into the elephant trap of 'extras'.

COPING WITH 'COWBOYS'

Here your management skills will be stretched and tested. The Office of Fair Trading receives around 60,000 complaints annually on home improvement matters, of which a good 20,000 are to do with double glazing. That figure must be the tip of a very unhealthy iceberg. There are perennial suggestions for some sort of official control of builders' standards—the authorised builders would have some kind of identifying badge—but this seems remote. The best advice must be that if a job requires planning permission, building regulations control and the services of an architect, you may be wise to avoid a 'cowboy builder'. Always go for the reputable, long-established firm even if it means paying more.

'Cowboy' builders are, quite simply, those builders who work in the 'black economy' almost exclusively for cash, are one step beyond the reach of the taxman and are never registered for VAT. They live very much from hand to mouth but because they do not have overheads (they do not pay tax, and only go in for the bare minimum of paperwork) they can theoretically quote cheaper rates than their straight colleagues. They tend to trade on the ignorance of the general public as to the true value of the work they do, and are not above charging old ladies £100 to replace a washer in a cold tap. Some get so far above themselves and are so accustomed to charging rip-off prices that their quotes are even higher than those of their straight colleagues. They tend not to be able to work to building regulation standards and blanch with fear at a District Surveyor the way Dracula would at an approaching crucifix.

In theory, of course, there is no reason why a brick laid, or a pipe plumbed by a cowboy should be done any better than by a straight builder; and it must be said that some cowboys are cowboys through choice—because they would rather not pay tax; while some have the status thrust upon them—they are just not very good builders and do not have enough clients to warrant the running of a properly organised business.

Compare cowboy quotes with quotes from properly accredited builders. If you are getting the sort of deal that you cannot refuse (by comparison with the VAT inclusive prices of the straight builder) then it may be worth taking the risk. But enter this relationship with your eyes wide open.

That does not mean that you will be giving the cowboy a free rein, so to speak. The simplest and only way of controlling such builders is to make clear that you will be making payments in arrears. There is really not much point in going beyond that. You can assume for instance that the cowboy will be uninsured and that the phrase 'defects period' would not be part of his vocabulary. Because they are dramatically undercapitalised cowboys will often not have enough money to start your job up and may well ask you for some cash 'in front'. Explain that only to the extent of buying in materials specifically for the start of the job are you breaking your cardinal rule of only making payments in arrears for work done.

Straight builders normally add a small margin on to the cost of materials to cover the expenses of 'porterage' (transport) and time spent in obtaining them. Again, if you take over the job of buying materials you will find that it will work out much cheaper. If possible, take the builder with you to the builders' merchants so that he can point out precisely what he needs. Alternatively, if you do not have time for that, tell the builder you will pay for materials once he produces a receipt for them. But never hand over cash for materials unless your relationship has developed into one of genuine trust.

Cash on the nail Such will be the straightforward nature of your relationship that cash on the nail will be required at the end of the job, and any reluctance to come up with immediate payment in full will be interpreted by the cowboy as extreme bad faith.

To put it mildly, it is not in your interests for your relationship to deteriorate to this point.

Either the outcome is satisfactory all round and you and the cowboy part company on good terms; or some of the work is not up to standard and you are unhappy; or the cowboy is unhappy because you are withholding money, and if you paid him you would feel ripped off. If the work done is sub-standard then you will more or less have to take this on the chin—there is no reasonably practicable way of getting a cowboy to return to a botched up job and put it right. Indeed you may not want him to anyway—he may just botch it up even more.

In the last instance, where the cowboy is demanding excessive payment (either for a bad job or just because it is excessive) you have an instrument of persuasion on your side which, if used carefully and if he is sensible, will back him off smartly: you are in a position to play the Inland Revenue card.

For the cowboy this is the ultimate deterrent, or the financial equivalent of a powerful kick in the groin. The one thing all cowboy builders have in common is that they are fugitives from the Inland Revenue and are not registered for VAT, and since you will have their home address and telephone number you can blow the gaffe on them.

It is usually best to take a diplomatic approach. Tell the cowboy that you would in the normal way of things try to claim tax relief on the money paid to him, and that if you did so, you might be asked to supply his name and address, which might have repercussions for him in the Inland Revenue and VAT areas of his financial anatomy. Of course, if he was prepared to be reasonable about his excessive cash demands, you would see what you could do, and you might do him a favour and undertake not to reveal his name to the Inland Revenue.

Everything depends on how you put this across, but you may well find that your cowboy suddenly turns into a model of the reasonable man. If the relationship deteriorates, however, and threats of any kind are made, then do not hesitate to inform him that he will find himself in Wormwood Scrubs (or any appropriately local slammer) so fast he will not know what hit him.

SPECIAL FORMS OF AGREEMENT

There are two forms of agreement specially designed for your protection. Get these forms from any law stationer. The JCT (Joint Contracts Tribunal) Agreement for Minor Building Works is much used by architects, and includes all the necessary clauses. It is ideal for most building work under £100,000, and for use where you employ one contractor to carry out the whole job.

The NHBC (National House Building Council) publishes a standard form of agreement which essentially comprises a guarantee by the seller/buyer that the house has been or will be built properly and that if any defects appear within two years of completion of the work they will be put right.

The real value of this agreement is that, on its signature, the NHBC itself issues the buyer with an insurance policy covering against loss if the builder goes bankrupt during the job or during the guarantee period so that defects cannot be put right; and cover against the appearance of major structural problems (shifting foundations) and damage resulting from it from the end of the two year guarantee period up to ten years from completion of the works.

The rights of the buyer can be passed on under the NHBC agreement to any subsequent buyers provided any defects which appear are reported as soon as practicable by the then owner. Notification of the first appearance of a defect (for instance, a minor crack in plaster work) would be sufficient notice to enable a subsequent owner to claim under the guarantee, and the insurance policy, if the cause of that crack turned out to be a major underlying defect such as shifting foundations. If you are a 'subsequent buyer' it is as well to check before you buy the house whether the seller has notified any defects which have appeared.

The NHBC scheme is voluntary and builders cannot be forced to participate in it. But there are two good reasons why it is in their interest to become NHBC approved builders. First, the NHBC guarantee and insurance policy makes a house or converted flat that much easier to sell; and second, the builder's liability is also limited by the insurance policy—after the initial two year guarantee period the buyer is required to claim under the insurance policy first and set any money recovered under the policy against the amounts for which the builder might have been liable. So there is something in it for builder as well as buyer.

WHOM CAN YOU SUE WHEN A DEFECT APPEARS?

Virtually everybody, you will be relieved to hear, provided certain conditions are satisfied. First of all, though, a word about the real world. Builders and general tradesmen have an uncanny knack of disappearing or becoming bankrupt, or may be well protected behind the armour of a limited company, and with all the rights in the world you may find yourself fencing at shadows. Court actions are uncertain and expensive. You will also be required to 'mitigate your loss' in so far as you can, and may be on dangerous ground if you refuse any offers to rectify defects unless it is quite clear that the problems are major, and beyond the capabilities of the original workmen.

Having said that, you have a number of arrows in your quiver.

Builders as well as suppliers of any goods which builders may use owe you a duty of care in respect of any work done, building materials used or any goods installed into your house, and this applies whether or not you are the original owner or purchaser, or an owner further down the chain of ownership. You have a statutory period of six years from the time the defect was discovered, or ought reasonably to have been discovered, to bring your action for damages. Take the example of a builder you employ to put up a kitchen extension on to your house; two years after the building works are complete, the foundations begin to shift. The six year period begins to run not from the completion of the work but from the point you noticed signs of foundation movement. Also, let us say, the builder installed a boiler which blew up and caused damage. If you could show that the boiler had been incorrectly installed, you could sue the builder; and if you could prove that the boiler itself had some defect, you could sue the supplier the builder bought it from.

The Defective Premises Act 1972 specifically imposes a general duty on anyone taking on work for or in connection with the provision of dwellings (houses, flats) to see that work is done in a workmanlike or professional manner with proper materials so that the dwelling will be 'fit for habitation' when completed. Builders are obviously covered, but so are architects, surveyors, sub-contractors such as electricians and plumbers or any specialist the builder decides to use, as well as suppliers of custom-made goods.

You do not have to have a direct contractual relationship with the builder (or other professional) to sue under the Act and it is quite sufficient for you to have bought an interest in a house (or flat) which was newly built (or converted) though make sure that the work was done after the Act came into force on 1st January 1974.

The Act seems to cover all professionals with the possible exception of the building inspector, but the courts have since developed rights under the general law of negligence to cover these people, and so it will be, for example, that the local authority will be liable to you if its (district surveyor) building inspector failed to exercise reasonable care in inspecting foundations for compliance with building regulations.

It may seem unfair, but if you buy a house or lease a flat which turns out to have defects the person you may feel most aggrieved and angry with, the vendor of the premises or the landlord (if you are a lessee) will be the one person you cannot sue for negligent building work. In one case a concrete canopy over the front door of a house fell on to the occupier. The builder was liable for negligent building work but the occupier's landlord could not be sued.

But there is an exception, if the person from whom you bought the house or flat was also the builder or developer, in which case you can sue them. You can, of course, have all the rights in the world but if the person you are after has no funds, or is bankrupt, or is a limited company with no assets, then forget it. This is not an area for the DIY lawyer, and if you get in this deep you ought to seek professional legal advice.

Call out rates for emergency services

Twenty-four-hour plumbers and electricians are listed in the Yellow Pages. Odd hourly rates are likely to be more expensive, but, nevertheless, call-out charges should never be more than £25 and the rate for the first hour's work should never exceed a further £15 for emergency plumbers and electricians. (EETPU, the union representing plumbers, recommend a £25 call-out rate plus payment for hours worked.) Watch out for rip-off call-out rates (some are as high as £30) and ask in advance whether any will be charged and if so how much. Always try to establish the rate in advance.

Where there are disputes, remember that it is much easier to tell a plumber that you are refusing to pay the excessive call-out fee if he is employed by a large company (you can say you will be taking the matter up with his boss), than it is to dispute a sum outstanding with a self-employed person, whose desire to see the sum paid may be altogether greater and more immediate. So, wherever possible use established businesses (they will be well used to client disputes) rather than self-employed cowboys who have been known to undo the work they have just done when clients refuse to pay their high rates.

Never pay in advance and wherever possible always test the work done before payment is made.

15

PLANNERS

Like all enforcers of unwelcome laws, planning officers are shouted at and roundly abused by members of the public on a daily basis. They spend far too much time for their own good 'just carrying out orders.' Nor must it be forgotten that city planners, acting under the protective mantle of legal authority, were responsible for devastating the centres of our major cities during a 30-year reign of architectural terror beginning in the fifties. And they are not above victimising the little guy, or in the case of an elaborate mud hut built in the back garden of an East London house, impressive West African ladies. I am, however, glad to report that Bill Heine, the owner of the celebrated Oxford Shark (a shark sculpture protruding twenty feet or so above a house in Oxford as a permanent reminder of the unusual possibilities of life) appears to have won his case; the enraged planning authorities are now suing the Department of the Environment for coming down on his side.

Planning officers are a dull breed and are customarily deadpan in their dealings with applicants. If you get excited they will simply tell you that their job is to implement planning policy and to take decisions purely on the basis of planning criteria. The Golden Rule must be never to lose your cool with a planning officer, until, of course, your application has been decisively rejected by the planning committee. Then you can go berserk. Your time will come.

You may need planning permission in a number of circumstances:

- you may want to extend your house;

- you may buy land with a view to building an entirely new house on it;

- you may want to buy a house to split into more than one dwelling, or if it already consists of flats, to turn it back into a family house;

- you may own land which would enormously increase in value if you could get permission to build houses on it.

BIG BROTHER IS WATCHING YOU

Planning matters are regulated by statute (The Town and Country Planning Act 1990 as amended by the Planning and Compensation Act 1991) and by government diktat in the form of circulars and 'structure plans' which are approved by the Department of the Environment; and most important nowadays, 'local plans' which have been elevated to the status of primacy in the interpretation of structure plans. The result is that government policy does percolate down to the grass roots of local planning applications, and may therefore affect any plans you may have. In effect, if your plans differ from the local plan, it is going to be extremely difficult, this side of the High Court or Planning Appeal, for them to prevail.

At the time of writing the atmosphere is generally favourable towards the granting of planning permission and the government's attitude towards development is that there should be a presumption in favour of development unless there would be 'demonstrable harm to interests of acknowledged importance'. So loose is the wording of this that local planning authorities are able to interpret it endlessly to justify their decision on local issues.

An application is sent first to the local planning department which takes a look at the 'local plan' (drawn up from the structure plan which in turn has been approved by the DoE) to see whether there are any fundamental objections to the development proposed. Broadly speaking, areas are zoned either for business (B1); general industry (B2); residential; agricultural; or some other environmental designation such as green belt or area of outstanding natural beauty. If you make an application for permission to build a house in an area which the local authority has decided should be used for industry or agriculture, the planning officers advise the Planning Committee to reject it and permission will be refused on these grounds alone. But this is by no means the end of the line. You may have to remove the building and comply with the 'steps to be taken' part of the notice, which in other cases may mean that you have to restore the building to the condition it was in before you began work.

On appeal against a refusal of permission the government's relaxed view is much more likely to prevail provided, of course, there is some merit in your case.

Never start building work until you have checked with the planners to see whether you need permission. The planning officers should be able to tell you immediately whether you need permission or not, and if the case is borderline, or if they tell you that you do need permission and that it would be refused, arrange an appointment to talk it over. Even if no planning permission is needed you are not entirely off the bureaucratic hook—it may well be that the work you propose will still have to conform to Building Regulations and be supervised by the District Surveyor.

If you do need permission then eventually you will need to draw up plans, which will usually involve the services of an architect. But there is nothing to prevent you from making the preliminary overtures to the planning department; try to be reasonable and get the planning officers on your side.

OUTLINE AND DETAILED PERMISSION

Planning permission comes in two forms: 'outline' and 'detailed'.

Outline is really to do with the principle of whether building work should be allowed to happen at all, and not much attention will be paid by the planners to the details of what you propose, (although plans will have to be submitted to show the extent of the work).

One of the planners' main concerns will be the density of any proposed development and it is at this stage the number of houses on any particular site will be decided upon; or, in the case of a house to be divided into flats, the number of flats.

Detailed permission requires a much more refined set of plans. The particular layout of any proposed units will be fixed, taking into account 'means of escape' (fire regulations) as well as matters of style, decoration, permitted building materials, and question of access and parking. In addition to all this there will doubtless be 'building regs' to take into account—see page 164.

WHEN DO YOU POSITIVELY NEED PERMISSION?

• For any proposed works involving **change of use**. If you are thinking of buying a warehouse to convert into loft apartments, check to see whether it will involve a change of use from 'business' to 'residential'. On this point alone planning permission would be essential and not necessarily easy to obtain. Change of use also includes converting a single residential house or flat into more than one unit. So if your plan is to buy a family house and make three flats out of it you will be caught by the 'change of use' trip-wire and will need planning permission.

• For any work which will involve a change in the **external appearance** of your house. This would include building a front wall or putting railings up.

• Any work which involves building of any kind of new **permanent structure** will need planning permission. Here we are talking anything larger than a potting-shed. Certainly a prefabricated pebble-dash garage (even assuming you would want to build such a thing) would need planning permission. If in doubt, ask.

• Any addition or **extension** to your house which will add to the gross cubic area of the property by **more than 10 per cent** needs planning permission. Anything less, and no permission is required. So you might be able to get away with that new bathroom on the ground floor, or a conservatory extension to your living room, but inevitably any work done will have to be subjected to the gaze of the District Surveyor, the Environmental Health Inspector and will have to conform to the Building Regulations.

Planning permission is **not** usually required for internal work— so relax if you have in mind the creation of a 'through' lounge, or the removal of a chimney breast. If the work involves structural alterations, however, you ought to let the district surveyor know. You still have a responsibility to keep within the building regulations, and the district surveyor will want to satisfy himself that whatever you do to the building does not render it structurally unsound and a danger to people who are wandering about inside.

PLANNING PROCEDURE

Planning procedure begins with:

• a (sometimes lengthy) negotiation stage with the planners;

• the formal application, which generally takes at least six weeks but sometimes as long as three months before it is considered by the Planning Committee.

• the Planning Committee will consider the application along with the recommendations (if any) of the Planning Officers which are usually (though not always) adopted;

- a decision is reached and reasons are always given;

- the result may be entirely positive, positive with certain conditions, or negative. In either of the last two circumstances it is open to you to appeal to the DoE to get the decision reversed, a lengthy and sometimes expensive procedure on which you should take professional advice from a solicitor versed in planning procedure. Appeals can involve written submissions (this you could do yourself), which are much less expensive than the £2000 a day you should set aside for any hearing at which you are represented by a planning barrister.

Negotiating with the planners

If the planning officers have made a genuinely perverse recommendation to their committee (they are not above this) they can be broken and humiliated on appeal.

Find out how it was that your application was refused. It is not beyond the bounds of possibility that the planning officer was on your side and the committee went against you and flew in the face of their own planning officer's report; and in these circumstances it has been known for planning officers to give evidence against their own committee and strongly in the applicant's favour on appeal. If you get on reasonably well with the planning officer you increase the possibility of this happening.

The aim of your dealings with the planning officers is to secure their positive recommendation for your proposals. If it is clear at the start that they have an entrenched hostility to the scheme because it offends some principle, find out whether the principle is a basic one (if it is you are looking at an appeal) but if it is less than fundamental, examine every possibility of compromise. Ask them to suggest the sort of scheme they would not object to.

Ask them whether anything you could suggest *would* gain their approval. If the answer is no, you are on a loser—you will not get a recommendation and any application you make is likely to be rejected. If there is a scheme they would approve of, ask them what it is. They will not play cat and mouse for ever. Then begins the horse-trading often best conducted by an architect—which should result in your getting some of the things you want and the planners getting their way on other matters.

Do not get the impression that you must pander to the planner's every whim. Short of positive approval and a glowing recommendation to the planning committee lies an area of more or less neutral ground. Here, the planner will tolerate your proposal without going overboard to recommend it to the committee. The proposal may be good in parts, from the planners' point of view, so that your application may receive a qualified recommendation, and at the end of the day, the committee might decide to grant planning permission, but impose some conditions of its own, such as on types of material used or a limit on the time period for which it remains valid (planning permission usually lasts for five years).

Interested parties

Interested parties are generally given 21 days to lodge an objection against a planning application. The planning officers have to put these before the committee, but if they approve of your application they generally advise the committee not to take the slightest notice of the objections. Equally, if the planning officers think the application should be rejected they will use any local objectors to support their views.

An interested party is not strictly defined but usually comprises owners or occupiers of adjoining property, local history groups and any quasi-official watchdog committees such as the Parish Council.

This is the time when local issues are suddenly invested with murderously high feeling and you discover that the neighbour you always thought was reasonably pleasant turns out to be a critical busy-body, motivated by envy, self-interest and a desire to impoverish you.

Try not to lose your cool or bribe anyone.

IF YOU BUILD WITHOUT PERMISSION

You may have gone ahead with works without planning permission by mistake, not being aware that you needed it. Do not panic. It makes sense to rectify the situation as soon as you can because for as long as the property has a planning defect it will be difficult to sell and your 'asset' will have been 'impaired'. You can apply for permission retrospectively and it will be granted if, in normal circumstances, it would have been granted. If permission is refused the planning authorities may tell you to demolish the offending structure. Again, no panic. You may decide not to comply, which is your prerogative, and in this case the authorities might serve an enforcement notice on you, requiring you to remove the structure. If you think you have a good case, or even if you do not, you can appeal against it. Only if you eventually lose this appeal do you run out of alternatives. You will have to restore the building to the condition it was in before you began work. In fact, provided you do not build anything too outlandish, the odds are in your favour that any building or added excrescence begun without planning permission will remain standing.

Try to resist any temptation to go ahead and start building without planning permission, even where there are good practical reasons—you may need to start work before winter weather sets in and it becomes impossible to dig foundations. If the application is uncontroversial then in all likelihood retrospective permission will be granted. Be careful, however, if it rubs planners up the wrong way and if your eventual application is problematic for any reason you may run the risk of total loss and have to pull down the structure you built. And the planning authorities have four years to take action against you to enforce any notice.

NATIONAL PARKS AND CONSERVATION AREAS

National Parks Planning Authorities were set up by Acts of Parliament to look after areas of outstanding natural beauty in England and Wales for the benefit of the general public, and one of their principal functions is strict control over building and land use.

They tend to be very sparing with their allocations of planning permission for newly built housing. Even in circumstances where an ordinary planning authority would immediately concede the point—for instance in applications for infill development involving a piece of open land which is surrounded by existing housing—a National Park Planning Board will turn down the application if it feels there is sufficient housing in the area and if it in any way contradicts the 'Park Plan'.

Decisions by National Parks Planning Authorities can still in the present climate be overturned on appeal—provided in all other respects you have a reasonably good case.

If your house happens to be in a conservation area or housing action area it is likely to work to your benefit rather than cause you any problems. Any application for planning permission will, of course, be subjected to the usual planning requirements, and you can expect the planners not to take kindly to any request to alter the outward appearance of a building in a conservation area unless the result would be a more authentic reflection of the original state of the building. But if the planners approve what you are doing, you can even expect financial assistance either from the local authority (provided it has the money) or from the DoE (which generally does have money) if your house is within a conservation area designated by the DoE as being of special interest. The planners will advise you on this.

LISTED BUILDINGS

Under the Town and Country Planning Act 1971, there is provision for lists to be made of buildings which are thought to be of special historic or architectural interest. The lists are kept by the DoE which relies for the most part on local authorities to pick out buildings in their area which they think merit inclusion, and the buildings are then divided into different categories.

Grade I is a very small category for buildings of outstanding national importance or rarity, Grade II for the rest, with a special category of Grade II* (starred) reserved for the most outstanding of these. Well over 400,000 buildings are listed but still, out of a total housing stock of around 23 million, they only account for under 2 per cent of all houses.

Apart from the kudos of living in a house which is officially recognised as being interesting (and this is an unquantifiable something which helps saleability) the main practical consequence of owning a listed building is that you will have to obtain 'Listed Building Consent' from the local planning authority if you want to carry out any works or do anything to it which would alter its character. And this will be in addition to any straight planning permission which you may need.

In and of itself, the fact that a building is listed does not give you an entitlement to a grant, although it may be the case that if the building is considered sufficiently important by English Heritage (the government quango set up to look after historic buildings) you could get some contribution towards the cost of structural repairs—usually something less than 50 per cent of the overall cost.

GRANTS

If you live in a conservation area, or a housing action area, or an outstanding listed building, then it may just be that you can get a grant for repairs or improvements from either local or central government sources.

Local government dishes out four different sorts of grants, some discretionary, some mandatory, but you will find that the generosity of any grant you receive will be influenced by whether or not the local authority has any money at its disposal. Several London Boroughs and many District Councils up and down the country are strapped for cash to the point of bankruptcy. It is, however, always worth trying.

Improvement grants are available to bring dwellings up to a reasonable standard, but they are discretionary and the criteria are left deliberately vague. In times of plenty you can get an improvement grant towards the cost of a conversion, but in any council cash crisis they are the first to be axed.

Intermediate grants are mandatory and are available to pay for any missing standard amenities, generally of a sanitary nature, such as baths, showers, hand-basins and loos.

Special grants are available for improvements to houses in multiple occupation where there is no immediate prospect of conversion. They are commonly granted to hostels or hotels which are in need of basic improvements with particular attention being given to sanitation and means of escape (to conform to Fire Regulations).

Repairs grants are awarded by local authorities in areas designated as housing action areas or general improvement areas. Again, they are discretionary and apply to general matters of repair. If your house has been neglected to the extent that the council has put a 'closing order' on it (which requires you to bring the premises up to an acceptable standard), you stand a reasonable chance of getting a repairs grant, provided, of course, the local authority has the money to pay you.

Where the grants are discretionary, account will be taken of your means and you may only expect a proportion of the costs of work to be met out of public funds.

Grants for historic buildings: English Heritage is the arm of central government which now has responsibility for awarding grants for the structural repair of particular buildings of outstanding architectural or historical interest, or to houses which the DoE has designated as being within conservation areas. The fact that your house may be 'listed' does not automatically qualify it for a grant from English Heritage, but it helps. The criteria are much stricter and the grants are therefore more difficult to obtain than grants from local authorities.

The building must be deemed 'outstanding', and you will have to show that you will not be able to meet the cost of repairs out of your own resources—so be ready to hand over confidential information relating to your income. Nor will a grant be given if you have taken over responsibility for repairs (whether by buying the freehold or taking on a lease or a tenancy) within the preceding four years unless you can show that your taking on the building represents the only chance of saving it and you obtained it at a nominal cost or at a very low price.

Grants for structural repairs to historic buildings do not cover alterations, improvements, redecorations or maintenance but, having said that, it is possible to obtain a grant towards the cost of repair of items of furniture, paintings and other furnishings which are historically associated with the building, and even a grant towards the cost of upkeep of a garden and anything in it of particular interest, such as a folly.

Watch out for the standard condition that if you sell or dispose of your interest in the building within ten years all or part of the grant may be reclaimed. Nor should you start work until the grant has been fully approved; and take note that grant applicants will be expected to obtain three competitive tenders for carrying out the work. And when the work is complete, you should know that it may well be a condition of the grant that you open your house to the public on at least 28 days during the summer months.

Very rarely will a grant from English Heritage cover more than 50 per cent of the estimated cost of repairs, although this figure can be increased in cases of particular need or urgency. When you do get them, though, the grants can be sizeable—no application for any amount of less than £10,000 will be considered.

RED TAPE

16

BUILDING REGULATIONS

WHY WORRY?

Architects and builders call them 'Building Regs'. The bald facts are that any building not built, altered or converted according to the rules risks being demolished, and any builder (and this could be you if you decide to project-manage your scheme) is liable to a fine of £500 for what is a *criminal* offence plus a daily fine of £50 for every day the building remains in contravention of the rules.

Even if you are not your own builder, it will be no consolation to you that the builder's head rather than yours is on the block—any disruption of the building schedule could cost you money and at the end of the day you may be left to put the building right yourself or, at the very worst, the building could be demolished altogether (a rare occurrence, but possible). So, particularly if you decide to do without an architect, you must be able to ask the builder the right questions.

The whole question of whether building regulations or by-laws have been complied with will come up under the local land charges search. Your goal is to get the inspecting official to certify that everything is okay. If, when you come to sell your house, the vital documentation is incomplete, your chance of getting a good price, or selling at all, could be ruined. The stakes are high here and there is regrettably no quick way through the jungle. Do not take shortcuts.

The scope of the building regulations is wider than planning permission. As a general rule all building work requiring planning permission also requires building regulations approval, but not all work requiring building regulations approval also requires planning permission. So if you built an extension on to your house of less than 10 per cent of the house's gross area, you would not need planning permission (under the 10 per cent exemption rule) but you *would* need building regulations approval in the normal way.

London and the provinces

We now have a system whereby building in the capital is controlled by one set of rules, and building anywhere outside is controlled by another. In London the details of construction are to be found in the copies of the London Building By-Laws and are supplemented by the London Building Acts (a whole series of acts passed since 1930), to which all twelve Inner London Boroughs together with the City of London subscribe.

Building work in the provinces is controlled by the building regulations deriving from the Public Health Act 1961. Eventually it is anticipated that the rules will be standardised, but until this happens there are marginal variations in building standards as between building work done in London and elsewhere. In practical dealings with officials of the two systems the chief difference lies in the greater power wielded by the District Surveyor in London as against his counterpart in the provinces.

Whether in London or outside a reasonably experienced architect should know exactly what the builder can and cannot get away with in dealings with the DS or any other local authority official. You might also reasonably expect a local architect to know the DS personally, and you should find out early on whether their 'working relationship' is a good one.

WHAT THE RULES COVER

The rules set out the minimum requirement in terms of measurements and weights (they are metric) and, where appropriate, detail the kind of materials to be used. If your proposed building work involves any of the following, which it is difficult not to, you will need building regulations approval (if in doubt, call your local authority and find out):

- Preparation of site
- Resistance to moisture
- Structural stability
- Safety in fire
- Thermal insulation

- Sound insulation
- Stairways and balustrades
- Refuse disposal
- Valuation and height of rooms
- Chimneys, flues, recesses, hearths, etc.
- Sanitary conveniences (WCs, lavatories, etc. shower rooms, baths)

Some structures are partially exempted from the rules—so for instance you may find that if you are building a greenhouse, potting shed or a detached garage the foundations will not have to be so deep as for a dwelling house. Again, if you contemplate any serious building work, call the local authority to find out what the building regulations position is.

PROCEDURE

The procedure operates through a system of written notices that must be served by the builder on the District Surveyor or (in the provinces) the inspecting official of the local authority when work is about to start, and thereafter as and when important work happens. To begin with, a complete set of plans and details of instruction and materials to be used must be deposited with the local authority or the District Surveyor as the case may be. The builder may be asked, where necessary, to supply calculations relating to loads, stresses and the strength of walls. (Clearly this is going to be beyond most 'cowboy' builders, and in practice it is always the architect's job.) You can generally expect an answer within five weeks, this period can be extended to two months by agreement. If the plans are rejected the notice must give reasons so that you can appeal to the minister.

When work is about to start the builder must serve a Notice of Commencement of Works and this applies both in London and elsewhere. The builder must give written notice not less than 24 hours (provinces) or 48 hours (London) before the foundations and drains are covered over. If the foundations and drains are covered before being inspected the builder will be expected either to open them up or to dig an inspection trench so that the work can be properly viewed. This can take time and, unless you are alive to what is going on, the builder will charge you extra. You should expect your architect and certainly your builder to be in constant touch with the inspecting officer of the DS so that site meetings can be arranged and the work can be properly inspected as it goes along. Be ready to ask the architect and/or builder all sorts of questions. At the beginning of the job you will want to know whether all the appropriate notices have been filed—the starting of works and the notice of completion of foundations or drains.

Towards the end of the job you must check that fire regulations have been complied with. The inspector will want to see that:

• proper 'half hour' (the time they will hold back a fire) self-closing fire doors are in place;

• that any staircases are properly insulated against fire;

• that the drains have been tested and passed;

• and that the place is properly ventilated (the rules are strict about lavatories and internal bathrooms).

The job of supervising the building work is sometimes shared by different inspectors, so you may find yourself making appointments with not only the DS or his provincial equivalent but a fire prevention officer and an 'environmental health inspector'—the 'drains' man.

ENFORCEMENT

If the various inspectors see anything they disapprove of they have powers at the 'approval' stage to prevent work from starting and once building work has begun they can stop it at any time. Beware, then, of 'Notices of Objection' or 'Notices of Irregularity'.

You will also find that before any certificate of compliance is issued—and this may be vital if you are selling any part of the building—you will have to pay the inspector's fees. These are based on the overall cost of works, but are to some extent negotiable. On building works worth £20,000, expect to pay the local authority a fee of £200.

The local authority has a period of six years in which to bring action to enforce compliance with the rules, and this period begins to run from the time the defect is or ought to have been discovered.

If you go ahead and build without the necessary approval, do not panic. If the work has been carried out with 'proper' materials in a 'workmanlike' way then in all probability you will not be far from complying with the rules and the building inspectors will issue their approval retrospectively. In the scale of criminal offences failure to comply with building regulations is not particularly serious and you may find that prosecution will not even become an issue unless you refuse to put right what you have built or unless you have deliberately flouted the rules for some reason of your own. In these cases the heat can come down, and you can expect the inspectors to behave at their bureaucratic worst.

The thrust of all this suggests that unless the work is really piffling you should employ an architect to deal on your behalf with the building control authorities as well as with the planners. If you find that you lose out because the builder has failed or refuses to comply with the rules then you should make sure—and a diligent architect should protect your interests here—that it is a term of any contract you come to with a builder that building regulations be complied with.

STREETWISE TIPS

Your architect ought to know these, but they will be useful for you to know to keep him up to scratch.

- In the UK we have the draughtiest houses in the so-called civilized world, and the standards of insulation are generally low. Even the building regulations leave a lot to be desired and you should always insist on a standard higher than the rules demand, with particular reference to insulation of pipes, roof spaces and wall cavities. Ditto noise prevention.

- There are some very obvious fire and safety rules that you should be aware of: electrical points should never be located too close to showers, baths, sinks and wash basins (danger of electrocution); expect the inspecting officer to insist on half hour fire doors on all internal doors and for the doors to be self-closing (noisy but safe).

- There must always be means of escape and any design not taking this into consideration will be summarily rejected. For this reason lobbies and passageways are all-important. You cannot, for example, have a room leading directly into others, and there must always be a lobby between a bathroom and a kitchen.

- Staircases are particular danger zones, not only because of their importance in cases of fire (they should always be insulated on the underside by at least two sheets of plasterboard) but because people fall down them and through the balusters, they cannot be too steep; and vertical rather than parallel balusters are required to prevent people slipping through the spaces.

17

INSURANCE

This is the sort of red tape that you would be wise to wrap yourself up in. Returning from a weekend away you find that one or all the following has happened:

- The central heating broke down and the pipes froze, unfroze, burst and flooded the place, causing a ceiling to cave in and turning the basement into an indoor swimming pool.

- The place has been burgled. The thief broke a window to get in, broke your favourite dinner service for no particular reason, and walked off with every available piece of jewellery as well as your video and stereo system.

- A slate fell off the roof and decapitated a passer by (not the burglar unfortunately) who turns out to be a high salary earner and you face a claim from his estate for damages.

This sends you scrabbling to your business drawer to find the insurance. You are going to need three types, and although they are in no particular order they are all three of them important:

(i) buildings insurance
(ii) contents insurance
(iii) public liability insurance.

You go to your buildings insurance policy to claim for damage caused by the flood; to your contents insurance and your buildings insurance (the burglar broke the window) for loss and damage caused by the burglary and to your public liability insurance to handle the claim from the deceased slate-victim's estate.

These three types of insurance are often taken care of by insurance companies under the heading of household policies and it is possible to get a three-in-one package deal.

If you have a mortgage the building society or bank will, in order to protect the security on their loan, insist on making sure that you have adequate buildings insurance, and will act as agents or brokers themselves (in this way they also corner the insurance agency fee). Your lender will not be in the least bit interested in whether or not you have contents insurance to cover the moveable items in your house, and this matter will be left entirely up to you to arrange.

Buildings insurance

This covers weather damage, which includes storm damage, and damage caused by flood (rivers engulfing the house) or burst pipes (much more common) caused by severe cold. Nowadays most policies also cover structural damage caused by movement in the foundations. Note that damage caused by wet or dry rot is not covered—insurance companies will tell you that they are insuring you against some unfortunate accident, and are not offering you a maintenance contract designed to halt the progress of some fungal disease. If your roof caves in under the weight of an excessive snowfall then unfortunately you are not automatically covered.

Each case would be considered on its merits and some insurers might take the step of having the house surveyed to make sure there was no possibility of weakness in the roof due to the occupiers lack of maintenance. If there was any hint of blame on the part of the owner, the claim might be refused or severely apportioned.

Frost damage is quite simply, and rather surprisingly, not covered by buildings insurance and nor, usually, is damage to fences and gates. Because of the increased fire risk thatched roofs are a specialist item of insurance for which the larger companies charge a premium. Try the Country Gentlemen's Association which offers a special low rate scheme for thatched houses.

Most buildings insurance policies are index-linked, which means that they will rise automatically every year in line with the retail price index. You would be wise to check that the amount of buildings insurance actually covers the value of the house—in a year in which house prices rise sharply the actual value could and often does outstrip the insurance value. Also check that the insurance covers the full replacement value of the buildings with no deductions of any kind.

Public liability insurance

This is generally included in buildings insurance, but if you have not seen a copy of the buildings insurance policy (because your lender has not sent you one) you should ask to see it to check that you are covered. The usual cover is up to £250,000 and the protection extends to any persons who suffer injury (or death) sustained while in your house, or as a result of being near your house (this would cover the falling slate scenario). It would also protect you from claims by trespassers—it may come as a surprise, but you are under a duty to take full steps as common humanity rights dictate to prevent harm befalling a trespasser. This would cover warning signs on building sites while your house was in the course of construction (although very arguably this would be the builder's responsibility anyway).

If you booby-trap your house as a preventative measure against burglars you might find yourself looking down the business end of an action for damages from the injured burglar. Ironically it is probably cheaper to kill a person outright in terms of damages payable, although in this situation the insurance company would probably refuse you the benefit of public liability insurance on the grounds that you had deliberately caused harm to a member of the public.

Contents insurance

This covers most but not all of the moveable objects in a household which are those that do not form part of the fabric of the house. An estimated quarter of the households in the country carry no contents insurance whatever. There are two bases of cover available in contents policies **indemnity cover**, where the insurance company will knock amounts off for general depreciation, and **replacement-as-new** cover, which means what it says, and is evidently worth more than indemnity cover. Establish whether your contents policy is indemnity or replacement-as-new, or whether, as is often the case, different items are covered on different bases under the single policy.

Events precipitating damages are: fire, storm, flood, loss through theft and, sometimes accidental damage. As a way of keeping down claims for trivial amounts, most policies knock the first £25 or £50 off each claim, but shop around and find one that provides full compensation.

MAKING A CLAIM

Contact your broker or the insurance company itself as soon as you can. You are under a duty to 'mitigate' (lessen) damage in so far as you can, so if you are, for example presented with a burst pipe, get a plumber to fix it. Similarly, in the case of storm damage to roofs and walls, get a builder in to put up a temporary cover (a tarpaulin) over the damage. Bills for emergency repairs are usually acceptable as part of a weather damage claim under contents or buildings insurance. In the case of a burglary, secure the building against the possibility of further entry, but expect to be closely questioned about the extent of your security arrangements. If you left the door wide open the insurers might take the view that you virtually invited the burglars in and scale your claim accordingly.

Claim for the full amount of any damage, and if you are in any doubt as to the value of what is damaged or lost, get a specialist assessor in. If for instance you have damaged antique furniture, get an antique dealer in to value it. If you have had jewellery stolen, describe it to a jeweller and get a rough assessment.

The case for keeping a household inventory is strong. You then know what you have lost, and you can have the whole lot valued periodically and upgrade your insurance if necessary.

Paying Out Provided there are no suspicious circumstances, insurance companies generally meet small claims without an argument. If your claim is for £1000 plus, you can expect a call from a loss assessor (also known as loss adjusters) who will have been called in and paid for by the insurance company purportedly to look after the interests of both parties, but in fact to investigate any claim, assess any loss, and find out if there are any circumstances (negligence on your part, or the damaged item being already in a worthless condition) which would enable the insurer to reduce the amount payable. Consult the Institute of Public Loss Assessors for a good local firm. The loss adjuster will call up to make an appointment and, if possible, you should keep any broken or damaged items to show them. You can expect the wheels of commerce to grind exceedingly slowly particularly in the aftermath of a burglary where, unless the items stolen are essential for the maintenance of civilised life (a cooker might qualify here), the insurance company will probably let you sit it out for a couple of months before coming up with the compensation. To be fair, they are usually quicker to act in severe weather damage cases.

Should the insurance company behave badly and if you have any trouble take your complaints to the Insurance Ombudsman Bureau. And on that bureaucratic note, we end.

GLOSSARY

Agents
A once successful species which did well in the High Streets of most towns at the expense of local populations of greengrocers and fishmongers. The male was more common than the female, but both sexes tended to have perfect teeth, BMWs and wide-lapelled jackets.

Sudden severe lack of wealth, on a scale never seen before, forced the species into irreversible decline.

Auctions
Property sales in which, in the heat of battle, you can part with more money than you expected for something you had not properly inspected.

Banks
Things that hold rivers in place, or places to get loans and mortgages.

Bridging loans
Pioneered by Telford, who took out the first bridging loan, literally refers to the sort of loan you need when you are required to construct a bridge; or a potentially disastrous loan from a bank, enabling you to own two houses at the same time for, you hope, a short period.

Chains
See old castles and Hammer horror movies.

Condominium
A term borrowed from Roman Law to denote a building block whose tenants own the building jointly. Not—as you might suppose—a biologically useless part of the upper intestine, easy to remove in a simple operation, and tastefully designed to leave almost no scar.

Contract races
Races to discover who can sign a contract the quickest, which happens when the heat is really on, and two or more people are after a property.

Conveyancing
This is what makes the world go round, and is the magic business of passing the legal title of a property from one person to another. A kind of dancing involving two or more people, and a lot of pieces of paper.

Duplex
Mouth fresheners, two-storey flats—that sort of thing.

Dutch Auctions
Originally referred to sales in which the price is slowly reduced until a buyer can be found. Now means a sale in which the price is talked up by an agent in a kind of private auction. And, who knows, it probably happens in Holland too.

ERM
Er . . . dunno.

Easements
An ointment for marathon runners? And positive or negative obligations that run with a property.

Freehold
The Zen wrestlers amongst you will immediately recognise this as the famous 'Freehold Lock' whereby you can freeze your opponent in his tracks with the concentrated force of your gaze. But for ordinary people like the rest of us, this is in fact the technical term for absolute ownership of property, not limited by a term of years.

Gazumped
'I've been gazumped' was Livingstone's unrecorded response to Stanley's famous question. Livingstone had just lost the film rights to *Out of Africa*.

Possibly comes from the Yiddish, *Gazeumph*, meaning, simply, to accept a higher offer on a house before contracts have been exchanged.

Gazunder
From Australian slang, meaning to throw up unexpectedly on someone's shoes. Hence the more general meaning of doing something unpleasant without warning, usually in circumstances in which the recipient has no option but to accept the situation gracefully.

Hard sell
Property, like any commodity, can be sold by unrelenting pressure—or hard sell. Those particularly at risk are impressionable first-time buyers.

House-Hunters Anonymous
A 12-step self-help group for people who spend their time fantasising about luxurious houses and making fruitless forays into the housing market.

Interest free
Describes the condition of intense relief at being able to make the monthly mortgage payments. Usually followed by severe depression when you realise you only have baked beans to live on.

MIRAS is the system of mortgage payments with tax relief built in. Oddly enough, this is available whether or not you pay income tax.

Joint Possession
Not just the possession of marijuana, this also involves the ownership of property by more than one person either as 'joint tenants' or 'tenants in common'. Delicate legal concepts best explained by your nearest solicitor.

Landlord
If you own a piece of freehold land you can call yourself one of these, if it pleases you.

Usually it is the nicest thing tenants (leasehold or otherwise) can think of to describe the person who owns the freehold of the flat or house they are living in.

Mortgage
A kind of lifeless greengage perhaps. But more of you would describe it as a millstone around your neck.

Negotiating
The best way to do this is not to do it at all. Be firm. And if you can't be firm, be clever.

North-South divide
The Offa's Dyke of the twentieth century, it stretches from the Wash to the Bristol Channel and effectively keeps the northern hordes at bay from their frightfully sophisticated southern compatriots.

Offer
The price you offer for a house. Or a proposal made to the prospective partner which may or may not be tender.

Party Walls
Unlike barn dances, party walls have nothing to do with enjoying yourself, and indeed if they enter your consciousness at all it will usually be as a source of irritation or expense. The usual definition is a 'wall or fence between two adjoining properties or houses'. Simple idea. Plenty of arguments.

Personal search
Usually conducted by Customs and Excise officers at your various points of entry and departure, a personal search is the sort of thing you may wish to carry out when the local authority cannot get its act together.

Principal Private Residence
A taxation term. Normally there is no difficulty in locating it—for most of us our Principal Private Residence (PPR) is the house we live in. But people with several houses may be put through the exquisite pain of 'electing' their country estate or their town house. Decisions, decisions.

Rate-capping
Referred to elsewhere in this book as the knee-capping of local authorities which, whether or not you think they deserve it, is what it amounts to.

Redemption Fee
At first sight you might think this is some kind of downpayment on accommodation in the hereafter (something of a speculative investment therefore). Much more mundane though is this charge, which is sometimes made when you pay off your mortgage ahead of time.

Seller's panic
The morbid state of mind of sellers who think their property will never sell and are grateful for any offer, however low it might be. Sometimes the panic is justified, in which case the condition is reactive; sometimes not, in which case it is neurotic.

Sitting tenants
Tenants who prefer to sit rather than stand. Usually they turn out to be sitting on a lot of money, if they play their cards right.

Staircasing
No, this is not the specialist business of constructing staircases. It is a radical new concept in housebuying involving the purchase of a house, step by step, until you own an entire staircase. You then go on to buy the bathroom, landing, living room and so on.

Tender offers
Very sensitive, loving offers? Like all such offers the recipient is not required to negotiate. See Chapter 4.

Unmortgageable property
Property on which you cannot get a mortgage, no less! But seriously, here is your chance to become a developer. Get a bank loan, buy it, and turn it into something magnificent.

Vacant possession
When you open the door of your new place and find that someone has got there before you, or indeed has not left, vacant possession is something you have not got. The golden rule has to be NEVER part with the purchase price until you are sure all the occupiers are out.

Woodworm

Grubs or larvae which bore into wood and enjoy an unvaried diet of the joists and timbers holding your house together. Okay, go ahead, kill them. But watch out for the militants—The Woodworm Liberation Front.

TABLE OF STATUTES

USEFUL ADDRESSES

Association of Consultant Architects
7 King Street, Bristol.

Banking Ombudsman
Citadel House, Fetter Lane, London EC4.

British Railways Board
Euston Square, London NW1.

Building Centre
Chenies Street, London WC1.

Building Employers Confederation
82 New Cavendish Street, London W1.

Church Commissioners
1 Millbank, London SW1.

Country Gentlemen's Association
Icknield Way West, Letchworth, Herts.

English Heritage
23 Savile Row, London NW1.

Federation of Master Builders
33 John Street, London WC1.

Forestry Commission
231 Corstophine Road, Edinburgh.

House Builders Federation
82 New Cavendish Street, London W1.

Independent Surveyors' Association
113 Westbourne Grove, London W2.

Institute of Public Loss Assessors
14 Red Lion Street, Chesham, Bucks.

Insurance Ombudsman Bureau
31 Southampton Row, London WC1.

Joseph Rowntree Foundation
The Homestead, 40 Water End, York YO3

Land Registry
Lincoln's Inn Fields, London WC2.

Law Society
113 Chancery Lane, London WC2.

London Housing Aid Centre
189A Old Brompton Road, London SW5.

National Association of Conveyancers
2 Chichester Rents, London WC2.

National Association of Estate Agents
21 Jury Street, Warwick.

National Federation of Housing Associations
175 Grays Inn Road, London WCI.

National House Building Council
58 Portland Place, London W1.

Office of Fair Trading
Breams Buildings, London EC4.

Ombudsman for Corporate Estate Agents
PO Box 1114, Salisbury, Wilts. SP1.

Royal Institute of British Architects
66 Portland Place, London W1.

Royal Institution of Chartered Surveyors
12 Great George Street, London SW1.

Save Britain's Heritage
68 Battersea High Street, London SW11.

INDEX

Gazumping 27, 28, 35, 37, 47, 59, 66-68, 88, 89, 121, 122
Gazundering 58, 68-69, 88
Gearing 77
General improvement areas 161
General rates 103
Germany 11, 12
Golden handcuffs (soft loans) 83
Grampians 56
Grants 162-164
Ground rents 49
Guarantees 26, 41

Hard sell 62
Heathrow 19
Heine, Bill 153
Hell's Angels 39
Heritables 33
Highlands, Scottish 56
Holiday lets 96
Home improvements 70, 71
Home improvements loans 102
Hotel bills, liability for 31
Hotels 19
Household policies, insurance 169
Household inventory 172
Housing action area 161
Housing Associations 13, 54, 55, 75
Housing Claims See Claims
Housing Stock 10
Hygiene 27

Indemnity 36, 69
Independent Surveyors Association 127
Inheritance Tax (IHT) 99
Inland Revenue 80, 98-104, 149, 150
Interest rates 80, 91, 92
Interest relief *See* Tax relief

Institute of Public Loss Assessors 172
Insurance 169-172
 against defaulting on mortgage repayments 83
 buildings 169, 170
 claims 171, 172
 contents 169, 171, 172
 exchange of contracts, and 110, 112
 indemnity cover 171
 leasehold flat 112
 life 83, 113
 public liability 169, 170, 171
 replacement as new 171

Johnson, Dr. 142
Joint agents, joint sole agents
 See Agents
Joint Contracts Tribunal (JCT) Agreement 149, 150
Joint Ownership
 of the freehold 49
 with housing association 54

Kitchens 72

Land Certificate 27, 114
Land Charges Department 111
Land Registry 23, 32
Landlord and tenant 93
Lands Tribunal 50
Law Society 108, 110
Lawyers 24, 25, 26
 and other conveyancers 106, 115
 See also Solicitors
Leasehold flats, insurance on 112
Leasehold property 27
Leasehold Tenants 21, 49, 112
Legal charge 75, 78
Legal title 25, 27

INDEX 189

defaulting on 80
Restrictions on use 26
Retentions on mortgages 127, 128
Right to buy 21, 49-53
    flats 49
    houses 50
    restrictions on resale 54
Rights of occupation, tenants 93
Rights of way 110, 114
Ronan Point 141
Royal Institute of British
    Architects (RIBA) 137, 139, 141
    condition of engagement 141
Royal Institution of Chartered
    Surveyors (RICS) 125

Sales 58-72
    private 60
    private, fast 46-47
    private, slow 40, 48
    reason for 38, 39
    synchronised 48, 59, 60
    timing of 59
Salisbury Plain 19
Saunas 71
SAVE Britain's Heritage 22
Scottish Highlands 56
Scottish Law 32
    deposits 33
    dues 33
    heritables 33
    missive of sale 33
    offers 33
    settlement 33
Scottish sales 45
    closed tender offers and 45
    negotiations in 45
Scottish solicitors 45
    solicitors' property centres 45
Searches 22, 24, 26, 43, 46, 69, 110, 111, 112, 113

building societies, and 28
    fee 28
    insurance 27
    personal 28
Scotland 33
    speed of 28
    subject to 28
Seller's panic 58
Selling 58-72
    hard sell, soft sell 62
Shared ownership 54, 55, 75
Shopkeepers 19
Shorthold tenancies 94, 95
Site visits 141
Sitting tenants 21, 41, 51-53
Soho 61
Solaria 71
Solicitors 26, 27, 29, 37, 47, 51, 68, 101, 106-115, 125, 141
    draft timetable 110
    estate agents and 109
    fees 107
    getting the best from 110
    insurance and 112
    preliminary enquiries and
    search 112-113
Scottish 45
Specification 144
Staircasing 54, 55
Stamp duty 102
Status enquiries 76
Sunday Telegraph 21
Sunday Times, The 21
Survey 126-134
    failed 127-128
    negotiations and 129, 132
    report 129, 130
    structural 36, 42, 131-133
    subject to 45, 47
    valuation 41, 64, 67, 76, 126-127
Surveyors 116, 126-134
    claims against 133